Mastering GMRS Radio

Your Complete Guide to General Mobile Radio Service Communication

Patrick Putnam

Copyright

Table of content

Introduction

More commonplace communication channels like cell phones and the internet frequently eclipse General Mobile Radio Service, or GMRS. However, GMRS is a lifeline for people who accept life's unpredictable nature, especially outdoor enthusiasts and disaster preparedness advocates. Its importance cannot be emphasized, particularly in the event of a failure of conventional communication networks.

Fundamentally, GMRS offers a dependable communication method that doesn't rely on infrastructure. In times of emergency, when cellular networks may become overwhelmed or rendered completely inoperable, this feature is extremely important. Imagine this: Just when you and your family are camping in the middle of nowhere, a storm hits. You must communicate with another group in the area or warn them of a possible danger. GMRS radios excel in this situation. They work using radio waves rather than cell towers or Wi-Fi, so you can communicate clearly and directly even in the midst of a chaotic environment.

Additionally, GMRS radios are designed to be user-friendly, which makes them perfect for both experienced and inexperienced communicators. They frequently have features like weather warnings and the ability to link to repeaters to increase range, which is especially helpful in places with mountains or dense forests where reception may be erratic. Because GMRS radios are so accessible, families can quickly include them in their safety plans and make sure that everyone is able to use them without needing a lot of training. The advantages of GMRS for outdoor enthusiasts go beyond crisis. Maintaining contact with loved ones can improve any activity, including hiking, biking, or just having a picnic in the park. Imagine having the assurance that you may check in with your loved ones at any time while mounting a rocky ledge and experiencing heart-pounding excitement. This is made possible by GMRS.

GMRS not only serves recreational purposes but also holds the potential to transform community safety programs. For example, neighborhood watch programs can use GMRS radios to communicate in real time. This improves the efficacy of safety precautions while also fostering a sense of community. Community members can better organize during events or emergencies by using GMRS, which keeps everyone safe and informed.

For GMRS communications, a wide range of people are the intended audience. Advocates for emergency preparedness are aware of how important it is to have trustworthy communication channels. They understand that every second counts during emergencies and that having a working radio could differentiate between pandemonium and well-coordinated action. The independence that GMRS offers, which enables individuals to explore the great outdoors while staying in touch with their group, is also valued by outdoor enthusiasts.

Throughout this book, what will you learn about GMRS? From choosing the appropriate tools to grasping the subtleties of successful communication, you will learn the basics. You will receive helpful guidance on how to set up your radio, comprehend its functions, and use it in different situations. Examples from everyday life will show how GMRS may be easily incorporated into your life, whether you're organizing a weekend trip or getting ready for an unanticipated crisis.

GMRS is essentially more than just a technical tool; it's an essential tool for people who value adventure, safety, and connectedness. By adopting GMRS, you provide yourself the tools to deal with both anticipated and unforeseen obstacles, making sure that you're never really alone wherever life leads you.

Chapter 1

Comprehending the Fundamentals of GMRS

General Mobile Radio Service (GMRS) Definition

More than just a fancy phrase used in radio circles, General Mobile Radio Service, or GMRS, is a lifeline that fills communication gaps when more conventional methods fail. Picture yourself hiking in the middle of nowhere, encircled by tall woods and the distant murmur of a river. All of a sudden, your cell phone loses signal, the clouds get darker, and a storm approaches. In this situation, GMRS excels, providing a dependable means of communication that may help you and your loved ones stay in touch when it counts most.

Definition of GMRS

Fundamentally, GMRS is a licensed radio service that uses particular radio frequencies to enable people to communicate over comparatively small distances. GMRS, which is overseen by the Federal Communications Commission (FCC) in the US, was created to make personal conversations easier, especially during emergencies. Users of GMRS benefit from higher power levels up to 50 watts which result in longer range and clearer transmission than Family Radio Service (FRS), which runs on lower power and does not require a license.

The Operation of GMRS

Ultra High Frequency (UHF) radio waves, usually in the 462 MHz and 467 MHz frequency ranges, are used by GMRS. These frequencies are ideal for short-range communication, particularly in metropolitan settings where signals may be disrupted by structures and other obstructions. GMRS radios are a flexible option for both outdoor enthusiasts and emergency preparation advocates since they can speak directly with one another or use repeaters to greatly increase their range.

Let's look at a practical case. Imagine a bunch of buddies going camping for the weekend. They can stay in continual contact while hiking over different types of terrain because they are equipped with GMRS radios. A brief message can notify the others if someone veers too far, protecting everyone. Having GMRS radios enables them to promptly organize rescue efforts or ask for assistance in an emergency, such as an unexpected weather change or severe injury, potentially saving lives.

The value of obtaining a license

There are obligations associated with using GMRS. Users are required by the FCC to purchase a GMRS license, which is now quite simple to do. In order to operate lawfully on GMRS frequencies, you must complete a straightforward form and pay a little cost. This step is essential since it not only maintains the channels' organization but also encourages users to take responsibility for their actions. In times of need, you want to be part of an organized network of communicators, not just another radio voice.

Why Opt for GMRS?

GMRS provides a fantastic disaster scenario solution for emergency preparedness advocates. When other means of communication are ineffective, GMRS might offer a vital channel during a local emergency or natural disaster. If a neighborhood group has a GMRS communication plan in place, they can quickly communicate important information like safety procedures, resource distribution, or evacuation routes in the case of an emergency. When every second matters, this kind of readiness can make all the difference.

Additionally, GMRS is quite beneficial to outdoor enthusiasts. Having a dependable way to connect with other hikers can make trekking in isolated locations more than just a fun activity; it can make it truly safe. Imagine if you and your companions choose to investigate a trail that meanders through untamed landscapes. In addition to adding a pleasant element—talking about the amazing views—GMRS radios guarantee that anyone who needs assistance or gets lost may get to the group promptly.

The development of GMRS

Since its beginning, GMRS has developed in tandem with technological breakthroughs. Early GMRS radios were modest, feature-limited machines that were mainly used for speech communication. Nevertheless, modern GMRS radios can be equipped with built-in GPS, weather warnings, and even Bluetooth. The increasing demand for adaptable communication tools that support contemporary lives is reflected in this progression, which makes GMRS a desirable option for both serious communicators and casual users.

GMRS's Development and History

The extensive history of the General Mobile Radio Service, or GMRS, reflects the development of communication technology in general. Its origins date back to the middle of the 20th century, when individuals were starting to understand how useful two-way radio communication was for both personal and professional purposes. The increasing demand for dependable, short-range communication among families, emergency responders, and outdoor enthusiasts led to the development of GMRS.

Larger, bulkier devices, such as CB (Citizens Band) radios, once dominated the radio communication environment. Although CB radios had their uses, their range was constrained, and their users had to follow stringent guidelines about power output and channel usage. The Federal Communications Commission (FCC) saw a market need as technology advanced: a service that could provide more range and improved functionality for both personal and recreational usage. GMRS was thus created. In order to enable users to operate on frequencies designated especially for private land mobile use, the FCC first created GMRS in 1960. GMRS was one of the first systems to combine the unofficial realm of personal radio communication with official regulations, as the original rules only permitted a certain number of channels and required users to obtain a license. In a profession that was growing quickly, this balance was essential to keeping things in order.

The emergence of family-friendly activities in the 1980s sparked interest in GMRS. Community gatherings, off-road excursions, and camping outings became frequent occasions where trustworthy communication was crucial. A wide variety of users were drawn in by the opportunity to stay in touch, make plans, and guarantee safety—from local businesses in need of a fast means of communication to families trying to stay in touch with one another to outdoor enthusiasts traveling to far-flung locations.

The technology increased in tandem with the need. The market was completely transformed with the advent of handheld GMRS radios. Even in places without mobile phone service, users were able to communicate over long distances thanks to these portable gadgets, which were frequently small enough to fit in a pocket. For proponents of emergency preparedness, this was revolutionary. When faced with an unexpected circumstance while hiking, having a trustworthy communication tool could differentiate between safety and mayhem. The regulatory environment changed as well. The FCC changed the regulations to permit additional channels and higher power outputs, which improved GMRS's utility even more. The license procedure was simplified by the FCC in 2010, making it easier for people to obtain GMRS for community or personal usage. A new generation of users was made possible by this deregulation, which further solidified GMRS's place in American communication culture.

Due in part to increased awareness of emergency preparedness, GMRS has seen a resurgence in recent years. Having a trustworthy way to communicate during emergencies is crucial, especially since natural catastrophes occur more frequently. For families and communities seeking to improve their emergency plans, GMRS radios offer a simple option. Imagine that neighborhoods using GMRS radios can coordinate relief efforts, communicate critical information, and keep in touch during severe weather events without relying on cell towers that could malfunction during a storm. GMRS is more important than ever today. Reliable connection is becoming more and more crucial as outdoor enthusiasts look for adventure in farther-flung places. With GMRS radios, you may easily communicate with your party whether you're camping at your favorite location, climbing a mountain, or exploring a deep forest. They are now necessary equipment for maintaining security and improving the whole outdoor experience. It is essential for outdoor lovers and disaster preparedness advocates to comprehend the origins and evolution of GMRS. It draws attention to both the cultural changes and technological developments that have influenced modern communication. GMRS is a movement toward a more cohesive, resilient society rather than just a tool. With its roots deep in the past and its branches reaching into the future, GMRS is well-positioned to play an important part in community and personal safety for many years to come.

Important GMRS features and advantages

When it comes to communication tools, General Mobile Radio Service (GMRS) stands out thanks to its special combination of features. Knowing its main features and advantages can make a huge difference for outdoor lovers and emergency preparation advocates, particularly in situations where being connected is essential.

The power of GMRS is among its most remarkable attributes. Generally speaking, GMRS radios use more power—up to 50 watts—than other services, such as Family

Radio Service (FRS), which has a 2 watt maximum. Under perfect circumstances, this increased power translates into a noticeably longer communication range, frequently reaching several miles. When hiking in a distant place with companions, having the ability to speak over a great distance could mean the difference between being lost and keeping safe.

The utilization of repeaters is another appealing aspect. Repeaters, which are stationary radio stations that receive a signal and retransmit it at a greater power level, are made possible by GMRS. Maintaining contact with family members or group members who live far away can be made easier with this feature, which can greatly expand your communication range. Imagine taking the kids camping and letting them explore on their own. No matter where they are in the area, a parent may easily check in and make sure everyone is safe by connecting a GMRS radio to a repeater.

Another important advantage is the privacy codes that GMRS provides. The Continuous Tone-Coded Squelch System (CTCSS) or Digital Coded Squelch (DCS) codes found on many GMRS radios help cut down on undesired interference from other users on the same frequency. This capability is very helpful in crowded places where a lot of people may be using GMRS frequencies at once, including at community events or in packed parks. By eliminating unnecessary chatter, users can concentrate on their talks, improving safety and clarity.

The robustness and adaptability of GMRS radios, which are specifically made for harsh outdoor operation, cannot be understated. Numerous types are weatherproof or resilient, which makes them perfect partners for outdoor activities like hiking and camping. Imagine trying to keep your company informed while navigating through an unexpected downpour; a dependable, waterproof GMRS radio can guarantee that communication doesn't break down when it matters most.

Additionally, GMRS radios are simple to operate, which is crucial for people who might not be tech-savvy. The majority of models have simple programming, clear displays, and easy-to-use controls. Fumbling with complex settings is the last thing you want to do when you're in a hurry. Whether you have a tech-savvy buddy or a family member who is less tech-savvy, anyone can quickly learn how to use GMRS radios due to their simplicity. The low entry cost of GMRS in comparison to other communication systems is yet another amazing advantage. There are no monthly costs or subscriptions needed to use the service once you have the proper GMRS license. Because of this, GMRS is an affordable option for families and groups who want dependable communication without having to worry about recurring costs. This cost factor is important when organizing a family vacation or an emergency preparedness plan.

In the end, adding GMRS to your communication toolkit boosts your self-assurance in handling a variety of circumstances. GMRS offers the dependable, adaptable communication solution you require, whether you're organizing a camping vacation with family, making sure everyone is safe during an outdoor activity, or just keeping in touch in case of an emergency. GMRS is more than simply a radio service thanks to its extensive feature set and useful advantages; it's a lifeline that helps you deal with life's unforeseen challenges and makes every journey safer and more pleasurable. Being proactive with safety and communication is what it means to include GMRS in your daily routine. It's about giving yourself and your loved ones the resources they need to deal with unforeseen circumstances so that every journey—whether it be through the difficulties of everyday life or into the wilderness—can be undertaken with assurance and tranquility.

Overview of Regulations and Requirements for Licensing

Understanding the rules and licensing requirements for General Mobile Radio Service (GMRS) is not only a formality; it is also an essential step in protecting your safety and the safety of others around you. Understanding the legal aspects of GMRS as an outdoor enthusiast or emergency preparedness advocate can help you make wise decisions and improve your communication tactics in emergency situations.

Let's start by discussing the most basic element: license. In the US, GMRS radios require a license from the Federal Communications Commission (FCC), in contrast to Family Radio Service (FRS) devices, which can be operated without one. Because GMRS uses frequencies that can travel farther than those normally permitted for unlicensed use, this licensing requirement is necessary.

How to Get a GMRS License

A GMRS license can be obtained through a reasonably simple and accessible process. This is how it operates:

1. Application: The FCC's Universal Licensing System (ULS) allows you to submit an online application for a GMRS license. This system is simple to use and walks you through the application process step-by-step. You must enter your name, address, and birthdate, among other basic personal details.

2. Fees: According to the most recent rules, obtaining a GMRS license requires a one-time payment of $70. You can renew your license for free after the ten-year period covered by this charge. The added safety and peace of mind that come with getting this license make the cost a little one.

3. No Exam Needed: Not having to pass an exam is one of the most alluring features of earning a GMRS license. This makes it possible for a wider variety of users, which makes GMRS a beneficial option for outdoor enthusiasts, families, and community safety groups.

4. License Scope: With a GMRS license, you can operate on particular GMRS frequencies, usually in the UHF band (460 MHz). All members of your immediate family are covered by the license; therefore, if your household has several users, one license will be enough for everyone.

Rules to Take Into Account

It's equally critical to comprehend the rules governing GMRS operation. Here are some important things to remember:

• **Frequency Limits:** Only specific frequencies are used by GMRS. It is prohibited and punishable by law to use any frequency outside of these designated ranges. Be sure to become acquainted with the particular frequencies shown on the FCC's GMRS frequency chart.

• **Power Restrictions:** The maximum power output that GMRS radios may produce is 50 watts. Nonetheless, a lot of portable GMRS radios usually run on lesser power levels, such as 1 to 5 watts. To optimize efficiency and range, take into account your devices' power output when developing your communications plan.

• **Repeaters:** GMRS repeaters are an additional option that can greatly increase your communication range. However, as there can be other rules involved, make sure to review the license requirements for repeater operation.

• **Emergency Use:** GMRS's capacity for emergency communication is among its most alluring characteristics. When conventional communication networks malfunction, GMRS can be a dependable fallback. Keep in mind that the FCC promotes the use of GMRS in emergency situations, so familiarize yourself with the relevant procedures.

Practical Use

Imagine if a friend gets an ankle injury while hiking far away. You need assistance, but there is no service on your cell phone. Your GMRS radio license and regulatory expertise come in very handy here. Help will arrive promptly if you use your GMRS radio to simply contact neighboring hikers or emergency authorities.

In addition to protecting yourself from legal problems, you also help create a safer communication environment for everyone by abiding by the rules and licensing requirements. Your dedication to comprehending GMRS and abiding by the law turns you from a simple user into a responsible communicator who is prepared to help in an emergency and build relationships in the wonderful outdoors. Understanding GMRS licensing and regulations is the first step to becoming a competent communicator in the dynamic field of disaster preparedness. With this information, you can handle obstacles and protect yourself and your family wherever your adventures take you.

Chapter 2

GMRS Radio Types

Base Stations, Mobile, and Handheld

Your communication experience with General Mobile Radio Service (GMRS) can be greatly impacted by the type of radio you select. Knowing the differences between portable, mobile, and base station GMRS radios gives you the ability to choose the best instrument for your needs, whether you're an outdoor enthusiast heading into the wilderness or an emergency preparedness advocate making plans for emergencies.

GMRS handheld radios

The most portable solution is a handheld GMRS radio, also known as a walkie-talkie. They are ideal for communicating while on the road due to their small size and lightweight design. Imagine walking through a thick forest with your loved ones and being able to talk into your radio by pressing a button rather than shouting into the distance.

The simplicity of using portable radios is one of their main benefits. The majority of models have simple controls and are built to survive the demands of outdoor activities. Features like weather notifications, which are available on many units, can be quite helpful during unexpected storms. Receiving a weather warning while camping, for example, may allow you to take shelter before the situation deteriorates. When choosing a handheld GMRS radio, take range into account. Under ideal circumstances, they can broadcast between 2 and 5 watts, with a range of 5 to 20 miles. But remember that this range might be impacted by weather, obstacles, and terrain. Take the radios hiking and observe how well they function in different types of terrain to test them. You will have a realistic understanding of what to anticipate in the field through this practical experience.

GMRS radios that are mobile

Because mobile GMRS radios are made to be used in cars, they're a good option for people who frequently drive great distances or go on group excursions. When compared to handheld devices, these radios have a much longer range because they usually have more power (5 to 50 watts). Imagine yourself and your friends driving through the mountains, communicating via your portable GMRS radio while you negotiate difficult terrain.

The majority of mobile radios only need a power source and an antenna that is put on the car, making installation very simple. Communication reliability is increased by this tight connection, which frequently results in stronger signals and crisper sounds. Additionally, a lot of devices have features like repeater capability, which lets you connect to nearby repeaters to increase your communication range even more. Mobile radios' adaptability might be very helpful to outdoor enthusiasts. Mobile radios keep you in touch whether you're collaborating with other campers or driving through national parks. Imagine being able to quickly update your party on evening plans as soon as you arrive at a campground.

Base Stations

With a larger wattage (usually 20 to 50 watts) and better performance for stationary transmission, base stations are the most potent option in the GMRS radio array. Base stations are a beneficial option for emergency preparation advocates wishing to create a dependable communication hub. They are frequently placed in residences or command centers.

Base stations are advantageous because of their improved features and range. Ranges of 20 kilometers or more are possible with correct installation and a powerful antenna, guaranteeing that you stay connected even under trying circumstances. This is especially helpful in emergency situations when coordinating rescue operations or conveying important information.

There are numerous real-world instances when base stations have been essential in the emergency preparedness community. Communities with base station radios, for example, can coordinate local resources and stay in touch with emergency services during natural catastrophes. Families can have a dependable way to communicate in the event of a power outage or other emergency by setting up a base station at home. Think about the site when establishing a base station. Installing your antenna on the roof or in a high spot can dramatically improve performance because elevation has a big impact on signal quality. Furthermore, spending money on high-quality components like a robust antenna and a dependable power source guarantees that your setup can handle the demands of any circumstance.

Making the Correct Decision

Your unique needs and situation will ultimately determine which GMRS radio type is best for you. Handheld radios are the best option if portability and usability are important to you. Mobile radios provide versatility and dependable communication for people who want additional power or who spend a lot of time traveling. Especially in emergency situations, base stations are perfect for building a robust communication network. Whichever kind you select, keep in mind that the objective is to improve your communication skills so that you and your loved ones remain safe and connected, whether you're on an exciting outdoor trip or in the event of an unforeseen emergency. Leverage the potential of GMRS technology and arm yourself with the necessary resources to successfully traverse life's uncertain terrain.

Important Features to Take Into Account

Battery Life, Range, and Power Output

Selecting the appropriate GMRS radio is an important decision that could affect your ability to communicate in an emergency or when on outdoor excursions; it's not simply about buying a fancy device off the shelf. Knowing important features like battery life, range, and power output will enable you to make wise decisions and guarantee that you have a dependable communication tool when you need it most.

Output of Power

One of the most important parameters to take into account is power output. It is expressed in watts, and in general, a radio with a larger wattage is more powerful. Models of GMRS radios usually range in power from 1 watt to 50 watts.

1. Low Power (1–5 Watts): Ideal for close-quarters communication, like between a few buddies when camping. A lower-power radio can be adequate if you simply need to communicate within a few kilometers. Since these radios are often small and light, hiking with them is simple.

2. Medium Power (5–25 Watts): For outdoor enthusiasts who might encounter a variety of terrain, this range is ideal. This power level can let you stay in touch over longer distances, usually up to 10 miles or more, depending on the terrain, if you're hiking or camping in an area with some barriers.

3. High Power (25–50 Watts): These radios are the mainstays of GMRS communication, with the longest ranges—often more than 20 miles—and the strongest transmissions. Advocates for emergency preparedness who wish to make sure their messages are widely disseminated will find them ideal. High power is your best buddy, whether you're off-roading and keeping in contact with family or organizing rescue teams after a tragedy.

Real-World Example: Picture yourself camping in the middle of a national park with your family. You have to call emergency services when a sudden storm hits. Your chances of getting through may decrease if you use a low-power radio because wind and rain might weaken the signal. By using a higher-power radio, you can communicate with other campers or emergency services who may be able to help you in addition to your family.

Range

Although range and power output are inextricably related, range merits its own discussion. It describes the range at which a radio can send and receive signals efficiently.

1. Recognize topography: Keep in mind that effective range is greatly influenced by topography. Signals can go farther in flat, open spaces, but they can be severely obstructed by mountains, woods, and buildings. In urban or heavily forested areas, a radio with a 20-mile rating may only function at a fraction of that distance.

2. Manufacturer's Claims: Always be skeptical of advertised ranges. Many manufacturers advertise maximum range in optimal circumstances, which are usually open fields free of obstructions. To determine realistic performance, it's a beneficial idea to test your radio in your typical setting.

3. Practical Advice: Think about how you will utilize the radio while selecting one for disaster preparedness. Make sure the radio has enough range to connect with nearby emergency services if your area is vulnerable to natural disasters. Choose a device with strong signal penetration if you often camp in steep terrain.

Life of the Battery

A dead battery destroys your ability to communicate more quickly than anything else. Various GMRS radios have varying battery life, which is affected by things like power output and usage habits.

Types of Batteries

1. NiMH (Nickel-Metal Hydride): GMRS radios frequently use these rechargeable batteries, which have a respectable lifespan but may eventually lose capacity.

Li-ion (lithium-ion): usually chosen due to their lighter weight and longer longevity. For regular users, they may be more costly, but they are worth it.

AA/AAA Battery Operated: Standard batteries are used by certain radios, making field replacement simple. When you are unable to recharge when off the grid, this can be a lifeline.

2. Estimated Usage: Throughout usage, monitor the battery life. Batteries will deplete more quickly at higher power settings. Consider purchasing a radio with a longer-lasting battery or a dual-power option that supports both rechargeable and conventional batteries if you anticipate going for extended periods of time without access to charging.

Real-World Example: Imagine yourself embarking on a strenuous hiking expedition. Your GMRS radio's battery indicator flashes red at night after a day of group communication. You can be separated from your buddies at the most critical moment if you didn't select a radio with a long battery life.

Features that can be compared include scanning capabilities and weather alerts

The features of the GMRS radio you choose can make or ruin your communication experience. Having a radio that suits your needs is essential for outdoor enthusiasts and emergency preparation advocates. Let's examine two crucial features: scanning capability and weather notifications.

Weather Alerts: Your Crisis Lifeline

Picture yourself camping in the middle of the tall forests when all of a sudden the sky grows gloomy. Rain was not mentioned in the forecast, but you can hear thunder rumbling in the distance. Weather notifications are useful in this situation. NOAA (National Oceanic and Atmospheric Administration) weather alerts on GMRS radios can save lives.

These radios provide real-time information on severe weather warnings, tornado watches, and flash flood alerts by continuously monitoring weather channels. To stay updated without continually checking your device, look for devices that can automatically switch to the weather channel when an alert is generated. For instance, the Midland GXT1000VP4's strong weather alert system makes it a favorite among outdoor lovers. It is ideal for those impromptu weekend vacations because it has 36 channels, an amazing 36-mile range, and NOAA weather warnings. You can make well-informed decisions about whether to set up camp or wait out the storm by being aware of the weather.

Capabilities for Scanning: Stay Up to Date

Let's move on to discussing scanning capabilities. Imagine being in the middle of nowhere when you hear someone on the radio talking about a forest fire alert. How do you keep yourself informed? Having a radio with strong scanning capabilities might help you stay focused. Your GMRS radio may cycle among frequencies while scanning, pausing on channels that are active and where discussions are taking place. In emergency situations where information is critical, this is very helpful. To make sure you don't miss any important information, look for radios with the Dual Watch feature, which allows you to watch two stations at once.

Take the BaoFeng UV-5R, which is renowned for its scanning power and adaptability. You can program this dual-band radio to scan GMRS and other frequencies, which will keep you in touch with emergency broadcasts and other nearby users. You can hear updates from other campers or emergency services thanks to this adaptability, which is quite helpful in emergency situations.

Comparing Features: Selecting the Best Option

Examine how these aspects complement one another while comparing radios. A complete safety net will be offered by a radio that can scan and send out weather notifications. Consider this:

• How frequently will I use this radio? Purchasing a radio with dependable weather alerts is a must if you enjoy hiking and camping frequently.

• Will I have to speak with people on a regular basis? If so, you'll stay connected with a model that has good scanning capabilities.

Let's apply this to a real-world situation. You're in the mountains on a hiking trip with several people. The weather radio on your GMRS radio warns you of an impending snowstorm halfway through. The weather alert feature on your radio allows you to swiftly reassemble with your squad and decide whether to seek shelter or return.

You and your group could have been in danger if you had a radio without scanning or weather warnings, although you might have been blissfully ignorant of the storm's approach. Combining these features increases your overall safety and gives you the ability to take action.

Examples of feature utilization in the real world

Examples of successful feature use in the real world might serve as strong motivators. Many campers and hikers depended on their GMRS radios with weather notifications to keep them informed during the 2018 California CampFire. Thanks to prompt warnings and radio communication with other outdoor enthusiasts, many were able to leave before the situation worsened.

These incidents highlight how crucial it is to spend money on a high-quality GMRS radio with necessary functions. In addition to improving your experience, the proper gear might be the difference between safety and danger.

Suggestions for Novice and Experienced Users

Whether you're an outdoor enthusiast planning your next excursion or an emergency preparation advocate outlining safety procedures, selecting the appropriate gear is the foundation of successful GMRS communication. Although there is a huge selection of GMRS radios and accessories, it is crucial to comprehend your needs and how each piece of equipment functions. Let's dissect this into useful suggestions for both novice and experienced users.

For Novices

If you're new to GMR, think about using a handheld radio. These versions are ideal for someone who needs a simple introduction to GMRS communication because they are portable and straightforward to use. Here are some suggestions:

1. Motorola Talkabout T600 H2O Radio

This sturdy, water-resistant radio is a fantastic place to start. Under ideal circumstances, it has a range of up to 35 miles and 22 channels. While hiking or camping, you'll be aware of any unforeseen weather changes thanks to the integrated NOAA weather alerts. You can concentrate on enjoying your time outside without being distracted by complex settings thanks to the easy-to-read display and straightforward button structure.

2. GXT1000VP4 Midland

With 36 channels and an amazing 36-mile range, this radio is a little more sophisticated but still simple for beginners to use. It is perfect for emergencies because it has an integrated lamp and SOS siren. Another game-changer is the weather alerts tool, which gives you peace of mind when traveling to far-off places.

3. Baofeng UV-5R

Despite being a dual-band amateur radio, the Baofeng UV-5R is very well-liked by GMRS users because of its low cost and many uses. Although it isn't as easy to use as the earlier options, it has more capabilities, including dual reception and configurable channels. You should research how to use it effectively.

For Experienced Users

Purchasing more advanced equipment is essential for individuals with some experience who wish to advance their GMRS communication. Features that improve range, dependability, and versatility are frequently given priority by advanced users. Here's something to think about:

1. The Kenwood TM-V71A

For consumers who require a lot of functions and outstanding power, this mobile radio is an excellent option. For serious communications, the TM-V71A provides exceptional performance thanks to its dual-band capability and integrated GPS. For people who spend a lot of time in cars or other immobile places where they can utilize its full potential, it's perfect.

2. The Yaesu FTM-400XDR

With a touchscreen interface and wideband reception, this is yet another cutting-edge mobile radio choice. You may share your location and get information from other users thanks to the integrated GPS and APRS (Automatic Packet Reporting System) features. For outdoor enthusiasts seeking dependable connection in isolated locations, it's ideal.

3. Outside antennas

External antennas can greatly improve your GMRS radio experience, regardless of your degree of skill. They can increase the range and clarity of your signal, particularly in forested or hilly locations where reception may be erratic. Seek out models that are compatible with base station and mobile settings, like the Diamond NR770HBNMO.

Add-ons That Make Your Experience Better

No matter your skill level, the following accessories can improve the effectiveness and enjoyment of your GMRS experience:

• **Earpieces and headsets** are essential for hands-free communication, especially in noisy settings or when engaging in outdoor activities. Compatible solutions from companies like Motorola and Midland enable distraction-free, crystal-clear audio.

• **Battery packs and car chargers:** It's important to keep your electronics charged, particularly during emergencies. Purchasing a high-quality portable battery pack or auto charger can guarantee that you never run out of power when traveling.

• **Waterproof Cases:** A weatherproof case can shield your radio from the elements if you're bringing it into the woods. For a secure fit, look for choices made especially for GMRS radios.

Practical Aspects

Consider the settings in which you plan to use your GMRS radio when choosing your equipment. For example, radios with great range and crystal-clear audio should be given priority if you frequently find yourself in deep forests. Likewise, if emergency readiness is your aim, look for devices with strong battery life and weather alerts.

The equipment you choose can literally spell the difference between keeping connected and being left in the dark! Imagine that a storm suddenly approaches while you and your companions are trekking. When you hear the weather alarm, you grab your trusty Midland GXT1000VP4 and decide to return before things get worse. In addition to improving your experience, the proper gear can save lives.

Chapter 3

Configuring the GMRS Radio

Initial Setup and Unpacking

Like opening a birthday present, unboxing your new GMRS radio requires a little dexterity in addition to enthusiasm and expectation. Your GMRS radio is no exception to the rule that first impressions count. When you carefully remove the packaging, you're uncovering more than just a gadget—you're uncovering a potent instrument that can improve your outdoor experiences or keep you linked in an emergency.

Examining the contents

Your GMRS radio will be inside the box when you open it, together with other accessories like a charger, an antenna, a rechargeable battery, and maybe a user manual. Examine everything for a while. Look for any missing pieces or obvious damage. Before you start setting up, make sure you have everything you need by doing a quick inventory. It's a tiny step that will help you avoid frustration later.

Getting to Know It

Get acquainted with the layout of your new radio before turning it on. Every port, dial, and button has a function. GMRS radios typically have:

• **Power Button:** This button turns the radio on and off and is usually found on the front or side.

You can browse through the various frequencies with the help of the Channel Selector.

• **Volume Control:** An essential function for clearly hearing transmissions, particularly in noisy settings.

• **Menu Button:** This brings up settings to personalize features like scanning modes or privacy codes.

As you look at these elements, think about how useful they are. For those who love the outdoors, accessibility is crucial. You may need to swiftly switch channels in an emergency or adjust the volume while trekking. These situations can go more smoothly if you are aware of your radio's layout in advance.

How to Charge Your Radio

Rechargeable batteries are included with the majority of GMRS radios. Make sure the battery is completely charged before you go. This guarantees optimal performance and equips you for any circumstance. Read the user manual to become acquainted with the features while charging. You may find things that can improve your experience that you hadn't thought of, such as an integrated flashlight or emergency alarm capabilities.

Consider purchasing additional batteries or a solar charger for those who are especially daring. In isolated locations with limited access to energy, these choices can literally save lives. Having a backup can be a source of comfort, particularly for those who push for disaster preparedness.

Setting up your radio

It's time to program your radio when it has been charged. Turning it on is the first step. The majority of GMRS radios offer an easy-to-follow setup procedure that lets you enter channels and frequencies. You may frequently enter the desired frequency directly into your radio if it has a keypad.

Pick your channels carefully

Choose channels that local emergency agencies or community organizations frequently use for emergency preparedness. Having this understanding can help you communicate more quickly in an emergency. Finding the correct group can improve safety and camaraderie during your outings, so outdoor enthusiasts should think about channels that other outdoor adventurers utilize.

Checking Your Configuration

Testing your setup is essential after developing. Look for a friend or partner to check in with. Use your radio to communicate over various distances to familiarize yourself with it and ensure its functionality.

Real-World Illustration

Imagine that you and your pals have chosen to part ways for a few hours while hiking in a national park. Effective communication skills can make a huge difference. By testing your setup beforehand, you can ensure everyone uses their devices and reduce trek fear.

Useful advice for achievement

• **Go through the handbook:** Although it may appear tiresome, the handbook contains invaluable information that can greatly enhance your experience. You'll want to have this resource close at hand for everything from advanced settings to troubleshooting advice.

• **Practice Makes Perfect:** You will gain confidence if you use your GMRS radio frequently in a variety of scenarios. To stay sharp, use it at neighborhood activities or on weekend excursions.

• **Pay Attention to Regulations:** The rules governing the use of GMRS vary by location. Learn about this to steer clear of needless penalties or issues.

Channels and Frequencies for Programming

The first step to efficient communication in emergency circumstances and outdoor adventures is to program frequencies and channels into your GMRS radio. Although it may seem difficult, it's as simple as putting up your favorite music once you understand the fundamentals. Knowing how to program your GMRS radio is crucial, whether you're an outdoor enthusiast looking for dependable communication on your next adventure or an emergency preparedness advocate hoping to stay connected during a crisis.

Recognizing channels and frequencies

Fundamentally, GMRS uses a set of frequencies intended for two-way communication. These frequencies are separated into channels, each of which serves a distinct function. Although GMRS radios normally have 22 channels, certain radios have the ability to reach more frequencies. The most frequently used GMRS channels are 1–7, which facilitate communication in both personal and emergency contexts.

Learn the frequencies that are accessible for GMRS before you start programming. Your user handbook usually lists the frequencies that correspond to each channel. Consider every frequency to be its own route. The right highway for your trip should be chosen even if you can travel on more than one.

A Comprehensive Guide to GMRS Radio Programming

1. Turn the Radio On: To begin, turn on your GMRS radio. On the front or side of the majority of devices is a power button. Make sure your radio's battery lasts long enough because low power can interfere with programming.

2. Enter Programming Mode: To learn how to enter programming mode, consult your user manual. Usually, this entails pressing a certain button or set of buttons. You can browse through choices on certain radios by pressing the "Menu" button.

3. Choose the Channel: To program a channel, use the up and down buttons to go through the available channels. For example, pick a channel that you all agree on in advance if you want to talk to pals while camping.

4. Set the Frequency: The next step is to set the frequency after choosing the channel. While some radios automatically configure the standard GMRS frequencies, others let you manually enter customized frequencies. Enter the desired frequency using the keyboard if your radio allows manual entry. Local radio organizations or outdoor forums can offer advice on popular frequencies in your area if you're not sure which ones to use.

5. Add Privacy Codes (CTCSS/DCS): Think about adding privacy codes to your channel if your GMRS radio allows it. Unwanted speech on the same frequency can be filtered out with the aid of these codes. Like a secret handshake, they only let people who know the code hear what you're saying. Just select a code from your programming menu's privacy code setting, then save it.

6. Save Your Settings: Look for the "Save Your Settings" option after configuring the frequency and any privacy codes. This is an important step since you will lose all of your hard work if you neglect to save. The majority of radios will beep or display a visual indicator to let you know that your settings have been saved.

7. Test the Channel: Now that everything has been programmed, a test run is necessary. To make sure your setup is working, find a friend who has a GMRS radio and check in. It's enough to say, "Can you hear me?" By testing your setup, you can make sure that everything is operational when you actually need to communicate.

Applications in the Real World

Imagine going camping in a far-off place with your family. You have the correct channels and privacy codes set up on your GMRS radios. Your youngest decides to go exploring one evening as night falls. Panic strikes at once—what if they are unable to return? However, you cry out for them using your GMRS radios. "Can you hear me, Emily? I've arrived at the campsite. Her voice crackles back, assuring you that she's okay and on her way back, and you feel a wave of relief. A pre-programmed radio can differentiate between pandemonium and peace in emergency situations. Cell networks may be overwhelmed during a natural disaster. However, you can speak with neighbors or emergency responders by using your GMRS radio, which is set to certain emergency channels.

Some Advice for Effective Programming

• **Plan Ahead:** Spend some time programming your radios prior to your outdoor excursions. Selecting shared channels should be discussed with your team. This guarantees that everyone is on the same frequency and prevents misunderstandings.

• **Frequent Updates:** Especially if you branch out into new areas, make sure to periodically review and update your programming. Local laws may change, or based on comments from other outdoor enthusiasts, you may discover more effective channels.

• **Keep the handbook close at hand:** Each GMRS radio is unique. During programming, keep your user manual near at hand since it serves as your guide to gadget mastery.

• **Remain Calm:** Don't freak out if you encounter problems. Breathe deeply and consult your manual's troubleshooting section.

No need to be afraid to program GMRS radio frequencies and channels. You can improve your outdoor experiences and be ready for crises with a little perseverance and practice. So go ahead and explore the world of GMRS and become an expert communicator!

Batteries, chargers, and antennas are necessary accessories

Your communication experience might be greatly impacted by the accessories you select when configuring your GMRS radio. Consider your GMRS radio the central component of your communication system, with chargers, batteries, and antennas serving as its essential organs. Making the correct accessory choices can increase your range, guarantee dependable power, and eventually give you the assurance to speak up when it counts most.

Antennas: Increasing Your Range

In the realm of GMRS communication, the antenna is frequently the unsung hero. It's what makes your signal powerful that it can penetrate barriers and reach considerably farther than your mobile device can. If you intend to use your radio in isolated areas, think about replacing the default antenna with a more potent model.

Antenna Types

1. Stock antennas: Included with your GMRS radio, these are suitable for basic functions but frequently have a short range.

2. Magnet-Mount Antennas: Perfect for mobile installations, these antennas may be mounted on the roof of your car to increase signal strength. They are easy to install and remove, making them ideal for outdoor enthusiasts on the go.

3. Base Station Antennas: Purchasing a high-gain base antenna can offer remarkable range if you want to put up a home base station. For optimal performance, these antennas can be installed on tall poles or rooftops.

Real-World Illustration

Imagine yourself camping in a national park. When the party breaks up to go trekking, you use your GMRS radio to set up a base camp. You can stay in touch with your buddies by installing a magnet-mount antenna on your car, which will improve your capacity to coordinate plans and guarantee everyone's safety. You can go extended distances thanks to the increased range, turning a straightforward camping trip into a planned excursion.

Batteries: Providing Energy for Your Conversation

Losing power when you need your GMRS radio the most is the most annoying thing ever. Choosing the right battery is essential, particularly for emergency preparedness advocates who require dependable communication during emergencies.

Battery Types

1. Nickel-Metal Hydride (NiMH): Due to their excellent performance-to-cost ratio, these rechargeable batteries are widely used. They are environmentally friendly because they can be recharged numerous times and offer dependable power.

2. Li-ion (Li-ion): A more recent alternative, these batteries have a longer lifespan and weigh less. They are popular among outdoor enthusiasts since they require less maintenance and have a longer battery life.

3. Alkaline Batteries: If you use your GMRS radio regularly, alkaline batteries might get expensive over time, even though they are practical for one-time use. However, in the event that you fail to recharge your rechargeable batteries, they provide a wonderful backup.

Useful Advice

• Regardless of the type you select, always keep extra batteries on hand. Since emergencies don't always happen on time, having backup power can be extremely helpful.

• If you're using rechargeable batteries, think about getting a battery management system to monitor the condition of your batteries. This guarantees that your battery is always fully charged before venturing into the wilderness.

Keeping your equipment ready with chargers

The battery in your GMRS radio needs to be charged, and how you handle this procedure can impact your preparedness in an emergency. Choosing the appropriate chargers and keeping up a charging schedule are crucial for both being ready for emergencies and having fun on your outdoor excursions.

Charger Types

1. Standard wall chargers: Usually included with your radio, these are simple devices. They may take a while to fully charge batteries, though.

2. Rapid Chargers: If you're pressed for time, rapid chargers can recharge batteries much more quickly, allowing you to resume your activities right away. These come in particularly useful if you use your radio a lot when on excursions.

3. Solar Chargers: A solar charger can offer an environmentally responsible traveler a sustainable means of powering their GMRS radio. They are quite useful when you are off the grid and away from conventional power sources, even if they might not charge as rapidly.

Practical Use

Imagine a situation where your camping excursion is interrupted by an unexpected storm. You have to get in touch with your friends fast because they are dispersed over the routes. You can quickly recharge your backup batteries using a rapid charger, guaranteeing that your GMRS radio is operational when it matters most.

Advice for Resolving First Setup Problems

An exciting first step in guaranteeing dependable communication during crises or outdoor excursions is setting up your GMRS radio. However, there are occasionally difficulties with the initial setup. In order to help you create a smooth connection from the beginning, this section offers helpful advice on how to resolve common problems you may run across.

1. Being aware of power issues

Power is one of the most common issues encountered when configuring a GMRS radio. Examine the power supply first if your radio isn't turning on. Have the batteries been charged? Make sure the rechargeable batteries you're using are inserted correctly and have enough charge. If the unit is mounted on a car, make sure the ignition is turned on and the power wire is firmly attached to the battery.

Real-World Illustration

Let's say you have just opened your new GMRS radio and are getting ready for a camping trip. Nothing occurs when you switch it on. You have a moment of panic, but then you remember to check your batteries. As it turns out, they are not seated properly. You can test the radio before you go by making a small adjustment that makes it come to life.

2. Positioning and connecting the antenna

Antenna positioning is another important consideration for the best radio performance. A poorly placed or improperly mounted antenna is frequently the cause of a weak signal. Verify that the antenna is positioned vertically and is firmly attached. When utilizing a mobile device, keep the antenna away from any metal items that can block the signal.

Useful Advice

Keep in mind that trees can block signals. Try moving to a more open area to improve reception if your radio keeps cutting in and out.

3. Errors in frequency programming

It can be intimidating to program your GMRS radio, particularly if you're not familiar with the device. Check your frequency settings again if you experience problems sending or receiving. Make sure you have the right channels programmed and that you aren't accidentally tuned to a restricted or inactive frequency.

An example of a scenario

Imagine yourself at a distant family gathering. Even with your radios set up, your family can't hear you. You have inadvertently selected Channel 5, which is designated for emergency broadcasts, according to a cursory review. The problem can be fixed by switching to the family channel, which enables easy communication as you spend quality time together.

4. Interference of Signals

Other electrical gadgets are one of the many sources of signal interference. Turn off any gadgets that are close by, such as Bluetooth speakers, Wi-Fi routers, or even other radios, if your radio is picking up static or you're having problems talking. Changing your location might sometimes help reduce interference.

Fast Fix

To evaluate whether signal quality improves, move away from your setup. This small change can frequently have a big impact.

5. Updates for firmware and software

Making sure your software is up-to-date is crucial for contemporary GMRS radios with digital capabilities. For firmware upgrades that can address bugs and enhance functionality, visit the manufacturer's website. Installing updates usually requires connecting your radio to a computer, so follow the directions.

Practical Use

After setting up your GMRS radio, you discover it doesn't work as promised. After a while of frustration, you see that a number of known bugs have been fixed in an update. Your radio operates properly after applying the update, highlighting how crucial it is to maintain your equipment up to date.

6. Consult user manuals and internet resources for advice

Never undervalue the importance of internet forums and user manuals. These resources can provide answers and insights on prevalent issues. Model-specific troubleshooting sections are frequently found on manufacturer websites. Joining online groups devoted to GMRS can also help you overcome obstacles by offering support and a wealth of shared experiences.

Collective Wisdom

Consider yourself stranded due to a programming fault. You find out that other users had a similar problem after looking through a forum. Their helpful advice and detailed fixes not only fix your issue but also help you become a better user of your GMRS radio.

Chapter 4

Improving Range and Signal

The Significance of Antenna Positioning

The location of your antenna can have a big impact on the signal's range and quality while using GMRS communication. It's more than simply a piece of gear; it's your link to other outdoor enthusiasts and your lifeline in an emergency. When you need communication the most, the proper antenna positioning might differentiate between a clear discussion and a jumbled mess or, worse, a total communication blackout.

Elevation should be taken into account first. When it comes to antennas, higher is nearly always better. Think about raising the antenna as high as you can if you're using handheld radio. Tall buildings emit signals farther beyond the horizon, much like a lighthouse beacon. Practically speaking, if you're trekking, locate a prominent viewpoint, like a mountaintop, where you may extend your antenna and set up your radio. Your communication range is increased by the elevation, which enables your signal to pass over obstructions like buildings and trees. Take into account the surroundings as well. Buildings, mountains, and dense vegetation can all reflect or absorb your signal, creating interference. Your signal can have trouble traveling even a few miles if you're in a dense jungle. It's crucial to place your antenna away from dense tree cover in this situation. In order to reduce interference from obstacles, try placing your radio on a rock outcropping or close to the forest's edge.

The kind of antenna you select is also important. Your communication range can be significantly increased with a gain antenna, which concentrates the signal in a particular direction. This makes it more dependable for emergency preparation advocates to call for assistance or collaborate with others. If you know you'll be in an area with plenty of obstructions or if you want to connect with particular groups over longer distances, you might want to invest in a Yagi or a directional antenna, even though a regular whip antenna might suffice in wide places. The orientation of the antenna is equally important. Depending on your communication requirements, antennas can be positioned either vertically or horizontally. Horizontal antenna orientations are best for long-distance transmission, whereas vertical antennas are usually preferable for connecting with nearby radios. Make sure your antenna is vertical and as clear of obstructions as you can if you're utilizing a mobile GMRS configuration, such as in a car.

Don't forget to account for ground plane effects as well. Performance may be impacted by the surface beneath your antenna. Your signal will travel farther if you're in an open field since the ground reflects some of the radio waves. However, your signal can be much weaker if you're in a valley or surrounded by tall mountains. Experimenting with an antenna arrangement in certain situations can provide unexpected outcomes.

A portable antenna mast can provide you with more height and flexibility if you like camping or other outdoor activities. A lightweight pole that you can elevate for improved communication and lower for transportation may be a basic configuration. Consider it your mobile communication tower; it's simple to set up and works well to boost your signal.

Participating in hands-on activities can also help you develop your abilities. Try positioning the antennas in various settings for an afternoon. Calling out to family members or other enthusiasts in different locations next to trees, on top of hills, and in clearings will test the range of your radio. You may learn about the subtleties of antenna arrangement and how it can significantly affect signal clarity through this practical experience.

Finally, remember to inspect and maintain your antenna on a regular basis. Eliminate branches and debris that could impede its operation. You'll be ready to stay connected in case of crises or exciting adventures if you have a well-maintained antenna. Gaining confidence and better communication are two benefits of realizing how important antenna placement is. As outdoor lovers and disaster preparedness advocates, it gives you more peace of mind to know that you can consistently connect with others. So go ahead and try different locations, raise your antenna, and relish the comfort of reliable connection wherever your travels take you.

Comprehending environmental and line-of-sight factors

Two essential components for successful GMRS radio communication are line-of-sight and environmental conditions. Gaining proficiency with these elements might be the difference between annoying static or dropped signals and clear, crisp communication, particularly in emergency situations or while out in nature.

Line-of-Sight: The Imperceptible Route

The unhindered path between your GMRS radio and your communication partner's radio is known as line-of-sight, or LOS. This idea is essential to radio transmission since any obstruction, such as hills, trees, buildings, or even the atmosphere, can weaken the signal. Speaking on your radio converts your voice into a radio wave that moves through the atmosphere, but it needs a clean path to get there. Picture yourself hiking through a stunning, untamed area. Eager to keep in contact with your group, you set up your GMRS radio. However, your connection weakens as soon as you pass behind a dense tree forest, and you are abruptly separated from your pals. This situation emphasizes how crucial it is to comprehend LOS.

Always look for the highest point in your surroundings to get the most out of your GMRS communication. Climb a little higher if you're in the mountains, and find a rise or a viewpoint if you're in a flat location. Your signal can reach farther when you are higher in the line of sight. To survey areas with high vision and few obstacles, use elevation charts and terrain maps.

Environmental Aspects: The Unnoticed Factors

Signal quality is also significantly influenced by environmental conditions. Take into account factors that can affect the propagation of radio waves, such as weather, vegetation, and urban structures.

1. Weather: Radio signals can become weaker due to scattering from rain, fog, and snow. Additionally, a "soggy" atmosphere caused by high humidity levels might weaken signals even more. It's a beneficial idea to be mindful that your communication may be less dependable during storms. By being aware of these limits, you can be prepared for situations where effective communication is essential.

2. Vegetation: Radio transmissions can be severely disrupted by dense woods or places with a lot of underbrush. Radio waves are absorbed by trees, particularly when they contain a lot of moisture, which is frequently the case in lush, green settings. The kind of terrain and the existence of natural barriers should be taken into account while organizing outdoor activities.

3. Urban Environments: Multipath fading is a phenomenon where radio signals bounce off concrete buildings in urban areas, causing confusion and signal loss. In these situations, open locations like parks or rooftops may be a better place for your GMRS radios to operate than within buildings or in between tall buildings.

Real-World Uses

Applying your understanding of line-of-sight and environmental considerations can improve your GMRS radio experience as an outdoor enthusiast or emergency preparation advocate. Here are a few useful tactics:

• **Scout Locations in Advance:** Do some study about the region you plan to visit before you leave. To see your position and spot possible signal obstructions, use applications such as Google Earth. If you intend to go hiking, consider the terrain you'll be walking on and modify your communication strategies accordingly.

• **Practice Communication Drills:** Arrange for your group to practice in a variety of settings. This can teach you directly how your signal is affected by various terrains. Try varying the height and position of the radio during these exercises to observe how it affects communication.

• **Pick the Correct Time:** Depending on atmospheric circumstances, signal quality can change during the day. Clearer communication opportunities are frequently available in the early morning or late afternoon. Keep an eye out for these trends, particularly if you depend on your GMRS radio for emergencies or outdoor excursions.

• **Use repeaters when needed:** GMRS repeaters might improve your communication range if you're in a difficult location with plenty of obstructions. Repeaters can get over some of the environmental restrictions by sending your signal through a higher point.

• **Keep Up with Weather Conditions:** Prior to leaving on a trip, always check the weather. You can foresee communication issues by being aware of possible weather trends. Make changes to your plans or be ready for restricted contact if storms are predicted.

Gaining a thorough understanding of line-of-sight and ambient conditions will help you improve your GMRS radio performance. Keep in mind that your ability to successfully negotiate these imperceptible channels and obstacles frequently determines how well you can communicate during crises or outdoor excursions. With this information at your disposal, you'll be prepared to handle any circumstance that arises and make sure your travels are connected, safe, and fun.

Methods for Making Effective Use of Repeaters

Repeaters might be the hidden heroes of GMRS communication, particularly for outdoor lovers and emergency preparedness advocates. They increase your signals' range by filling in any gaps caused by topography and the elements. You may improve your communication skills and make sure you keep in touch when it counts most by knowing how to use repeaters.

A repeater: what is it?

In essence, a repeater is a radio station that receives signals on one frequency and retransmits them, frequently with more power, on another frequency. Because it may greatly increase the range beyond what a portable radio could accomplish on its own, this is essential for GMRS communication. For example, depending on the topography and antenna height, a repeater can increase the range of a handheld GMRS radio to 30 miles or more, whereas a handheld radio may normally cover a radius of 1 to 5 miles.

Selecting the appropriate repeater

Take into account the following elements while choosing a repeater:

1. Location: Seek out repeaters situated on elevated terrain, including large buildings or mountains. The coverage region expands as elevation increases. Repeater locations and ranges are available in a variety of online sources.

2. Frequency: verify that the repeater uses a frequency that your GMRS radio can use. How UHF and VHF frequencies differ may also influence your choice.

3. License Requirements: In order to function, the majority of GMRS repeaters need a license. To ensure compliance, familiarize yourself with local rules.

4. Community Support: A few repeaters belong to a community network that offers extra assistance and resources. You can improve your experience and learn more about the finest repeaters to utilize by interacting with local radio groups.

Getting Ready for Achievement

Correct equipment setup is essential after selecting your repeater. Here are a few doable actions:

• **Accurate Frequency Programming:** Enter the input and output frequencies of the repeater in your GMRS radio. This guarantees that your signal travels to the repeater and returns on the appropriate channel when you transmit.

• **Use of PL Tones:** In order to gain access, many repeaters need a Private Line (PL) tone. The repeater cannot be accessed by unauthorized persons thanks to this tone. To determine which PL tone to program into your radio, consult the repeater's information.

• **Antenna Positioning:** Make sure your antenna is free of obstructions and as high as feasible for best results. For increased reach if you're in a car, think about installing a rooftop antenna.

Realistic Advice: Using Repeaters

1. Know Your Coverage Area: Become acquainted with the coverage area of the repeater. Spend some time learning about its limitations; signals might be impeded by buildings, slopes, and other obstacles.

2. Test Your Configuration: Send text messages from various locations. You should know your signal's range and quality. Make use of landmarks or other distinguishable locations as points of reference.

3. Join Local Groups: Get involved with GMRS clubs or user groups in your area. In addition to offering guidance and support, they can also provide personal experiences and advice regarding the use of particular repeaters in your region.

4. Maintain Clear Communication: Speak concisely and clearly when using a repeater. Keep in mind that several people can be attempting to connect simultaneously. Effective communication is maintained by adhering to radio etiquette and using common language.

5. Get Ready for Emergencies: Time is of the essence during emergencies. Before a crisis arises, practice using your repeater arrangement. Knowing your equipment and area repeaters can help you communicate important information more quickly.

Example from the Real World: A Trekking Experience

Imagine going on a hike in a far-off place with your companions. You've chosen a GMRS repeater with care to help your group communicate. The terrain starts to interfere with your handheld radios as you climb the mountain.

However, you can still talk to your pals who are farther down the route thanks to the repeater's reach. You decided to stop at the top and message a friend who remained at the campsite. You may communicate your location and check on supper supplies with a few radio taps.

A call regarding a lost hiker in the vicinity is later heard over the repeater. You can help coordinate efforts with local search and rescue teams because of your connections, which will ultimately contribute to a successful recovery. This case demonstrates the effectiveness of repeaters by turning a potentially difficult circumstance into a coherent, well-planned reaction.

Advanced strategies to increase signal strength

When it comes to General Mobile Radio Service (GMRS), a strong and consistent signal can mean the difference between seamless communication and complete frustration, particularly during outdoor activities or emergency circumstances. It's important to know how to maximize your signal power, which involves a combination of equipment, environment, and skill and goes beyond the radio itself.

1. Raise the antenna

Elevating your antenna is one of the easiest and most efficient ways to improve your GMRS signal. Obstacles such as buildings and topography can obstruct radio waves, which move in straight lines. You can greatly increase your transmission range by positioning your antenna as high as you can, such as on a tree, a tall pole, or even a roof.

Take, for example, a group of friends going trekking in a mountainous region. If they are in a valley surrounded by peaks, they can find it difficult to speak clearly. However, one member may be able to reach people far away by raising their GMRS radio with an external antenna fixed to a portable pole, preventing needless stress in the event of an unexpected separation or violent storm.

2. Select the best antenna type

Not every antenna is made equally. Your signal strength might be significantly impacted by the antenna you choose. Upgrade to a higher-gain antenna if you're using a handheld radio. By concentrating radio waves in a particular direction, these antennas improve clarity and range.

For instance, a basic 5/8 wave antenna may perform better than a typical 1/4 wave antenna. A directional antenna may be useful if you frequently travel through wooded areas where trees may disrupt transmissions. This kind of antenna reduces noise and distractions from other directions by sending and receiving signals mostly in one direction

3. Keep an eye on the frequency

Frequency is important in the world of GMRS. Depending on the surroundings, some frequencies may spread more effectively than others. For example, although higher frequencies may offer clearer signals but have a shorter range, lower frequencies tend to go farther but may be more sensitive to noise.

You can determine which frequencies are most effective in particular regions by experimenting with them during your practice runs. A little adjusting can produce better results, much as when you discover the sweet spot in your favorite radio station.

4. Pay attention to obstacles and terrain

Radio waves can be significantly impacted by terrain. Take into account the terrain when organizing outdoor activities. Are you surrounded by buildings, hills, or a lot of trees? These might block transmissions.

To reduce interference, for example, a team of disaster preparation advocates practicing in a forest should pick sites with unobstructed sight lines. Try to get yourself on higher ground whenever you can.

Additionally, removing physical barriers between radios can improve the quality of communication. Your signal is probably clearer if you can see your fellow communicator.

5. Make use of repeaters

Consider employing GMRS repeaters if you're in a place where direct communication is difficult. These gadgets greatly increase your communication range by receiving weak signals and retransmitting them at a larger power.

It can save your life to find neighborhood repeaters. Listings of repeaters in your area can be found on websites and in discussion boards. They can facilitate rapid communication with others in an emergency, offering crucial updates and assistance.

6. Conduct Routine Upkeep

Although it may seem insignificant, routine maintenance on your GMRS equipment can have a significant effect on performance. Verify that your batteries are in optimal condition, check cables for wear and tear, and check connections for corrosion.

One outdoor enthusiast, for instance, reported experiencing severe signal loss when camping. They discovered a loose connection at the antenna base after a brief examination. A straightforward tightening up allowed them to communicate again and prevented their hiking group from fearing isolation.

7. Use effective communication strategies

Strong signal strength depends on your communication style as much as the equipment. Make use of succinct, unambiguous words, particularly when under pressure. When transmitting, stay away from loud background noise and, if needed, select a quiet location.

Every second matters in emergency situations. Clarity and comprehension, when it counts most, can be ensured by practicing effective communication strategies beforehand.

8. Make quality equipment investments

In the end, purchasing high-quality GMRS radios can significantly alter the intensity of the signal. Choose models with more power, cutting-edge features, and positive performance reviews. This is an investment in your connectivity and safety, so don't choose the least expensive choice.

9. Gain knowledge through practical examples

Learning from the experiences of others has enormous benefits. One family, for example, split up when they encountered an unexpected downpour while camping in a rural area. They were able to immediately reconnect by using repeaters and elevated antennae as part of their preparation. They took the initiative to strengthen the signal, which helped manage a potentially hazardous situation.

Chapter 5

Best Practices and Communication Etiquette

Appropriate radio protocols making calls, answering, and talking

Knowing the correct protocol for utilizing GMRS radios is essential for efficient communication, particularly during emergencies and outdoor excursions. The manner in which you communicate over the air might mean the difference between safety and danger, as well as between clarity and confusion. Ensuring that everyone remains informed, composed, and connected is more important than simply adhering to the regulations.

Making Contact: The Art of Calling

There is more to communicating on a GMRS radio than simply hitting the button and talking. There is an obvious call sign at the start. You must introduce yourself before engaging in conversation. For example, if K5ABC is your call sign, say "K5ABC calling." This lets other people know you're attempting to get in touch.

The catch is that you shouldn't merely shout into thin air. First, listen! Make sure the channel is clear and unoccupied. By avoiding overlapping talks, this small gesture of civility may guarantee that everyone is heard. Think about this actual scenario: You and your pals are hiking when the weather unexpectedly changes. Checking in with another group is necessary. Take time to listen for any conversation rather than yelling, "Hey, is anyone there?" "K5ABC to Group Two, do you copy?" can be said with confidence after you've made sure the channel is clear. This conveys confidence and clarity in addition to respect for other people on the frequency.

In response: The Value of Recognition

Making a call is important, but so is responding well. You should swiftly answer the phone when someone calls you. Saying "K5ABC, I hear you" demonstrates that you have heard them and are prepared to interact.

Time is of the essence in emergency situations. The caller may feel more at ease if they receive prompt acknowledgment when a distress signal is issued. Imagine this situation: when you are camping, a fellow camper calls for assistance immediately because someone has been hurt. In addition to demonstrating that you are paying attention, a prompt and unambiguous acknowledgement sets the foundation for productive discussion of the matter.

To guarantee clarity, repeat important information if the circumstances permit. For instance, "Copy that" might be an appropriate response to the statement, "We need help at the north campsite; someone fell and can't move." K5ABC is on their way to the north campsite to provide support. This technique helps you concentrate on the particulars of the situation while also reassuring the caller.

Speaking: It's Important to Be Clear and Brief

Conciseness and clarity are your best friends while communicating over GMRS. Keep your communications succinct and direct. Aim for simple, unambiguous language rather than long explanations. Misunderstandings are reduced when language is used clearly. For instance, try saying, "K5ABC to Group One, we should relocate due to the storm threat," as opposed to, "I think we might want to consider moving our campsite because it looks like there's a storm approaching." This conciseness is especially crucial in high-stress scenarios where every second matters.

Radio transmissions in outdoor environments can be disrupted by background noise. Even with the sounds of nature all around you, make sure your message is easily perceived by speaking clearly and in a calm tone. Consider wearing an earpiece or headset that helps reduce distractions if you're in a noisy setting.

Using common languages and codes

To facilitate communication, many GMRS users employ standard codes, like 10-codes or Q-codes, in addition to being explicit. Although these codes may be useful, make sure everyone on your frequency knows about them. Confusion and, eventually, misunderstanding might result from using jargon that some people may not understand.

However, using codes isn't always required. The most effective language is frequently plain. It is crucial to use precise language that explains activities in an emergency. For example, state your actions explicitly: "I am moving to the east side of the lake to check for signals," rather than simply saying, "I'm going east."

It takes practice to get perfect

Practice is essential if you want to improve your radio etiquette. Bring your loved ones together for a radio training session. Create scenarios, such as someone getting lost and someone else having to plan a rescue. You can all gain a better understanding of appropriate etiquette and become more at ease with GMRS communication by role-playing these scenarios.

Joining regional GMRS forums or organizations is another option. Speaking with seasoned users might provide you with insightful advice on how to improve your communication abilities. You can develop a sense of community and gain a deeper understanding of appropriate radio etiquette by exchanging experiences and learning from others.

Knowing and applying abbreviations and codes

Particularly in high-stress circumstances like crises or outdoor experiences, effective communication can mean the difference between confusion and clarity. Using codes and abbreviations is one of the most useful tools you have. They facilitate communication, improve comprehension, and even foster user camaraderie. Every second matters while you're in the field or handling a catastrophe. Time-consuming explanations are the last thing you need.

The Value of Abbreviations and Codes

Codes and abbreviations are essential for a number of reasons. They

• **Improve Clarity:** A straightforward code may swiftly and effectively communicate important information over background noise or disturbance.

• **Save Time:** A few letters or digits can convey a whole idea or action when there are only a few seconds left.

• **Minimize Miscommunication:** Standardized codes lower the possibility of mistakes by ensuring that everyone is understanding the same message.

Frequently Used Codes

1. 10-Codes: These are abbreviations that are used to communicate information quickly. For instance:

10-4: Recognition (all OK).

10-20: Location (where are you?)

Situation of emergency 10–99

Although these codes may differ by location, knowing the fundamentals can be useful in a variety of circumstances. Imagine being on a hike with pals when you need to ask them where they are without yelling or raising any red flags. A straightforward "10-20?" can maintain the privacy of the conversation.

2. Phonetic Alphabet: This is necessary for clarity, particularly when communicating important details like names or coordinates. Similar-sounding letters can cause confusion, which is lessened by the phonetic alphabet. A brief reference is as follows:

A: Alpha

B: Bravo

C: Charlie

D: Delta

Saying "B as in Bravo" while communicating a license plate number that contains letters, for instance, guarantees that there won't be any miscommunication.

3. Morse Code: Although less frequently utilized in regular communication, Morse code can be extremely helpful in dire circumstances. In emergency situations, knowing how to send out an SOS (three short signals, three lengthy signals, three short signals) can save lives. "How would I ever use that?" you may ask. Imagine, however, that you have a flashlight and your GMRS radio fails. A brief sequence of light flashes could notify rescuers or other hikers in the area of your predicament.

Real-World Uses

• **Field scenarios:** Imagine this: You are camping in a secluded location when one of your group members is hurt. You could employ codes rather than hastily trying to describe the situation over the radio. At 10-20 (place), we have a 10-76 (an injury). I'm requesting help right away. This not only swiftly conveys the message but also maintains a composed and orderly tone.

• **Promoting Team Cohesion:** Team members feel more united when codes and acronyms are used. When everyone is in agreement, trust is increased and teamwork is enhanced. Practice utilizing codes in everyday discussions the next time you're out. When it comes to communicating under duress, this will become instinctive.

• **Customization:** Don't be afraid to work with your organization to develop your own codes. It might be quite helpful to set up special codes for particular situations, such as indicating that someone needs assistance without frightening other people. Just make sure that these codes are taught to everyone.

Things to Keep in Mind When Communicating

Communication is essential, particularly during outdoor activities or crises. Using a radio is about protecting yourself and others, not just communicating. When it counts most, knowing and implementing important safety precautions during conversations can make a big impact.

1. Select the appropriate channel

Consider yourself hiking through the bush when you need assistance. Your first step is to choose the right channel. There are several channels on GMRS radios, some of which are for general use and others for emergency communications. Learn which channels are most appropriate for local emergencies. Always be prepared by switching to the emergency channel and listening for responses if you find yourself in a tight spot. It may mean the difference between hours of waiting for assistance and receiving it promptly.

2. Make use of simple and direct wording

It's important to be clear. When you're under stress, whether it's from a storm that's coming or a partygoer who has vanished, your mind may be confused. Keep your communications succinct and direct. Rather than saying, "Can you come find us? I think we might be lost." Choose something more straightforward: "This is [Your Call Sign]." At a particular location, we are lost. I'm requesting help. This clarity makes it easier for people to comprehend your predicament and react appropriately. Keep in mind that the one on the other end may be dealing with their own stress.

3. Put safety before information

Although you may feel compelled to disclose your location and circumstances in detail, put your safety first. Prioritize communicating that message if you are in imminent danger. For instance, "Help! Saying, "We've encountered a bear!" is far more urgent than giving a detailed account of how it occurred. Keep your attention on the things that people need to know in order to help you.

4. The radio does not always function

Particularly in mountainous or densely forested regions, radios have limits. Be mindful that distance and topography might affect communication, even if you are comfortable with your GMRS radio configuration. Always have a backup plan. For example, as extra precautions, think about packing a satellite phone or a personal locating beacon (PLB) if you're in a very remote location. Having several channels of contact is always preferable when you're going somewhere new.

5. Create a check-in communication routine

Decide on a regular check-in time with someone who isn't traveling with you before starting any outside expedition. Tell someone when and how often you'll check in if you're exploring with friends. This way, the designated person will know what to do if you don't check in. For instance, they should notify the local authorities if you haven't contacted them by 4 PM and your scheduled check-in time is 3 PM. This tiny action could result in prompt rescue operations.

6. Remain composed in emergency situations

Maintaining your composure under pressure might be difficult. Panic, though, can result in inadequate communication. Before you speak, take a deep breath and consider your words. To guarantee clarity, restate important details if needed. Keep in mind that other people will rely on your capacity to speak clearly. Use your radio's fundamental features, such as indicating your distress if necessary, until you can effectively communicate your demands if you are having trouble expressing them.

7. Pay Attention to Other People on the Frequency

Many people frequently utilize radios, particularly during emergencies. Be polite when using a GMRS radio. Make sure the channel isn't already in use by listening before you talk. Wait until the other person has finished speaking before placing your call if you can hear them speaking. More efficient communication is made possible by this small act of attention, which helps to keep the frequency clear and in order.

8. Express gratitude thereafter

Remember to show your gratitude if you are fortunate enough to receive assistance. Saying "Thank you for your assistance; we're safe now" can make a big difference. It encourages a sense of camaraderie and solidarity among radio listeners in addition to recognizing the work done by others. Safety and connection are ultimately what everyone wants.

Emergency preparedness advocates and outdoor enthusiasts can greatly improve their enjoyment and protect their own and their friends' safety by prioritizing these safety factors when communicating. Effective communication can make the difference between a small nuisance and a serious problem in the unpredictable, changing outdoors or during unplanned emergencies. Always be ready, stay in touch, and keep safety as your top priority.

Instructions for Sustaining Unambiguous Communication

Effective GMRS radio use relies heavily on clear communication, particularly during crises or outdoor excursions where every word matters. Understanding the subtleties of radio etiquette might be crucial when communicating with friends, organizing with other campers, or transmitting important information in an emergency. These useful tips can help you speak effectively and clearly.

1. Make use of concise and clear language

It's easy to become agitated in a stressful situation. Don't use fancy words. Steer clear of technical phrases or jargon that could mislead your audience. Try saying, "I can't hear you well," rather than, "The signal is weak, and I can't establish a solid connection." Please say it again. This clarity guarantees that even if someone is agitated or distracted, they will understand what you're saying.

2. Consider Your Words Before Speaking

Much confusion can be avoided with a brief pause. Give yourself a moment to gather your thoughts before pressing the push-to-talk (PTT) button. Think about what information can wait and what is absolutely necessary. Clear and thoughtful communication can help avoid misunderstandings in emergency situations where quick judgments could be the difference between safety and disaster.

3. Determine who you are

Always state your call sign or your given name at the beginning of your transmission. Take "This is Camp Bravo," for example. Over. In addition to making it obvious who is speaking, this technique keeps the line of communication orderly and professional.

Knowing who is speaking might help listeners prioritize their responses and take appropriate action in tumultuous situations.

4. Make Proper Use of the "Over" and "Out" Signals

Clarity is essential in radio transmission. When you're done talking and ready for a response, use "over." Use "out" to indicate the conclusion of your message if you're finished and don't anticipate hearing from anyone else. When these signals are misused, people may become confused and wonder if it's their turn to talk or if you've disconnected. For instance, "I'm going to the lake for the evening; this is Camp Bravo." In contrast to "This is Camp Bravo, signing off," "Over" indicates that you anticipate a response. "Out." signifies that your communication is complete.

5. Engage in Active Listening

Talking is only one aspect of communication; listening is just as important. Make an effort to pay close attention to what other people are saying. Refrain from interjecting and fight the need to answer before the other person is done. Active listening promotes improved communication and shows respect. Use affirmations like "Copy that" or "Roger" to show that you're paying attention and digesting the information if you're in a group situation.

6. Pay Attention to Background Noise

Clarity may be hampered in outdoor environments by wind, wildlife, and other background noise. If you have trouble hearing or being heard, find a quieter place to be. Make sure everyone in the group is aware of the distractions from the surroundings. This understanding not only promotes clarity but also demonstrates your consideration for the demands of your team.

7. Remain composed and calm

During emergencies, emotions might run high. Maintaining a constant tone makes it easier to project authority and confidence. Before speaking, pause to take a deep breath if you are experiencing terror. A soothing voice can ease anxiety and give others a sense of security. Keep in mind that your manner sets the tone for communication; if you're composed, others will follow suit.

8. Make use of standardized signals and codes

Learn standard radio codes, such as the phonetic alphabet (A for Alpha, B for Bravo) or the ten-codes (e.g., "10-4" for acknowledgment). These standardized signals reduce misunderstandings and are particularly helpful in noisy settings or in situations where background noise is prevalent. Being aware of these codes can help you communicate more effectively and keep things organized, particularly in big gatherings.

9. Verify and repeat

To make sure you comprehend, repeat back any vital information you are given. For example, "Your message was received by Camp Bravo. I take it that you're suggesting that we meet at the north door at 3 PM? This procedure keeps important details from falling between the cracks and helps guarantee that everyone is in agreement.

10. Perfectionism comes through practice

Effective radio communication becomes better with practice, just like any other talent. Plan emergency drills or training sessions with loved ones. Play out situations where effective communication is essential, such as planning a walk or handling an emergency. In addition to boosting self-esteem, these drills acquaint everyone with the tools and protocol.

Example from the Real World: A Camping Trip

Think about a camping vacation where it's critical to communicate clearly. Your group must choose between packing up and waiting out a sudden storm that is approaching. Following the aforementioned instructions, the group leader announces, "This is Camp Alpha. There will be a storm soon. We have to make a decision soon. Over. Using their call signs, each member answers, repeating back important details to ensure comprehension. The decision-making process becomes productive, transparent, and serene, demonstrating how positive communication may result in safer and more pleasurable outdoor experiences.

You will be well on your way to becoming an expert in GMRS communication if you adhere to these rules. Clear communication will not only improve your experiences but also keep you and your loved ones safe, whether you're planning for emergencies or engaging in leisure activities.

Chapter 6

Procedures for Emergency Communications

The Value of Being Ready for Emergencies

It's not enough to have the ideal strategy or the appropriate equipment when a calamity happens; you also need to be ready to communicate clearly. Being prepared for emergencies involves more than just learning how to operate your GMRS radio; it also entails developing a thorough plan that can save lives and provide comfort in unforeseen circumstances. Imagine that one of your group members is hurt while you're trekking in a remote location with little access to mobile coverage. Panic strikes. Your ability to speak effectively and clearly at this time could differentiate between a quick settlement and a protracted crisis. This is where being ready for emergencies is important.

Recognizing the risks

Because emergencies can happen at any time, emergency preparedness is essential. Effective communication is essential in all situations, from personal crises like medical emergencies or becoming lost to natural disasters like floods and wildfires. Nearly 60% of all disasters are caused by weather, according to FEMA, and having a plan in place can significantly improve results.

Consider the devastating effects of the 2018 California wildfires, which ravaged the state. Communication failures made the mayhem worse and caught many individuals off guard. Individuals with emergency plans and dependable communication tools, such as GMRS radios, were able to contact emergency services, safely evacuate, and communicate with their loved ones. In addition to improving safety, preparedness increases community resilience.

Creating a Communication Plan for Emergencies

1. Evaluate Your Hazards

Determine the possible hazards in your area first. Is your area at risk of flooding? Are there frequent earthquakes or wildfires in your area? Knowing these dangers enables you to adjust your emergency communication plan to the particular difficulties you might encounter.

2. Define Roles for Communication

Assign members of your group to communication roles. Who will be in charge of contacting emergency services? To family members who are not around, who will communicate information? Confusion during a crisis can be avoided by assigning these responsibilities beforehand.

3. Establish a Tree of Communication

Create a communication tree that specifies who should get in touch with whom in case of an emergency. This arrangement guarantees the effective flow of information. If you're camping with a group, for example, you may assign one person to inform the group leader, who would subsequently get in touch with emergency personnel.

4. Select Dependable Equipment

Selecting the right communication tools is essential. GMRS radios are superior to conventional cell phones, especially in rural locations where service could be spotty. Make certain that everyone in your company has received training on the features and restrictions of these devices. Keep in mind that practice makes perfect.

5. Put your plan into practice

The difference might be enormous when emergency scenarios are simulated. To practice using your GMRS radios and according to the defined communication strategy, schedule training sessions with your crew. Everyone can feel more at ease and assured in their positions through role-playing.

The Journey of a Family in Preparation

The Smith family lives in a hurricane-prone area. They made the decision to take emergency preparedness seriously after seeing the destruction caused by Hurricane Katrina. They made an emergency communication plan, bought GMRS radios, and practiced frequently.

They were prepared for Hurricane Harvey in 2017. The family members dispersed throughout the state in search of protection as the storm grew worse. They were able to coordinate their operations and make sure that everyone was secure because of their plan, which allowed them to stay in contact via their GMRS radios. The Smiths felt powerful and in charge, while others found it difficult to connect in a trustworthy manner.

Remaining knowledgeable and flexible

Being informed is another essential component of emergency preparedness. Follow local emergency services on social media and sign up for weather notifications. Understanding real-time updates can help you modify your communication tactics as circumstances change, and knowledge truly is power.

Additionally, maintain your flexibility. Since emergencies rarely go as planned, it's critical to have a flexible communication style. Be prepared with backup communication methods in case the primary one fails. This could involve other platforms like social networking, text messaging, or even a scheduled meeting location.

The Community's Lifeline

Community resilience is a component of emergency preparedness that goes beyond individual protection. Neighbors might serve as crucial lifelines during emergencies. Practice community drills, form neighborhood communication groups, and build relationships with people in your immediate vicinity. Everyone can react to crises more skillfully if your community is stronger.

For example, neighborhood organizations were established to exchange resources and knowledge during the 2020 pandemic. Good communication was essential to keeping communities informed and safe, whether it was feeding the elderly or giving them real-time updates on local health precautions.

Concluding remarks

Emergency preparedness is a proactive strategy that includes identifying hazards, creating trustworthy communication channels, and cultivating a preparedness culture. It is not just a box to be checked off a to-do list. Your dedication to positive communication as outdoor enthusiasts and disaster preparation advocates can have a big impact on both your own and other people's safety.

Take the time to develop a strong communication plan. An otherwise chaotic scenario can become a well-managed response if you are prepared to handle emergencies. With GMRS radios in hand and a well-thought-out plan, you'll be able to confidently, clearly, and resiliently traverse the uncertain terrain of emergencies.

Formulating a Communication Strategy for Diverse Situations

Developing a strong communication plan is essential for emergency preparedness, particularly for outdoor enthusiasts. A well-planned approach can differentiate between chaos and successful crisis management because emergencies can happen at any time.

Recognizing the Value of a Communication Strategy

Picture yourself and your friends going camping. A calm evening is one in which laughter abounds and the fire crackles quietly. A violent storm is brewing on the horizon as black clouds suddenly roll in. Without a communication strategy in place, panic can strike rapidly. Even in difficult circumstances, a well-structured strategy ensures that everyone understands their job and how to relate to one another by providing clarity and direction.

Evaluating your requirements

Evaluating your particular needs is the first step in developing a communication plan. Think about the kinds of activities you plan to engage in, such as hiking, camping, or even boating. Every activity has different communication needs and possible hazards. For instance, what would happen if someone got hurt or lost while hiking in a distant area?

To begin, make a list of situations that might interfere with communication. Here are a few such emergencies to think about:

• severe weather conditions, such as floods and storms

• Emergencies related to medicine (injuries, allergic reactions)

• Missing people or groups

• Equipment failure, such as GPS or radio issues

Determining duties and positions

As soon as possible scenarios have been discovered, assign roles and tasks to your group. In an emergency, everyone should know who to call and their roles. For instance:

• **Team Leader:** In charge of communicating with emergency services and making general decisions.

• **Communicator:** The one responsible for operating the GMRS radio and other communication tools.

• **First Aid Responder:** qualified to manage medical crises by providing basic first aid training.

• **Navigator:** Maintains group location and makes sure everyone is aware of the evacuation path.

By assigning these responsibilities, communication is streamlined, and everyone is aware of what to do in an emergency.

Creating channels of communication

The channels you'll utilize for communication should also be covered in your communication plan. Cell service can be erratic in many isolated locations. GMRS radios can bridge this gap, but their proper use requires established procedures. Here are some pointers:

• **Selecting a Frequency:** Choose a major frequency that your group will utilize. Make sure that everyone's radios are set to the frequency. Having a backup frequency is also a good idea in case the primary one gets crowded or interfered with.

• **Check-in Times:** Set up consistent check-in times, particularly for outdoor pursuits like hiking. Decide to check in every hour, for example. Our procedure ensures everyone is present and helps identify issues early.

• **Emergency Signals:** Establish unambiguous emergency signals. For instance, "I need help" or "I'm injured" could be indicated by a certain sequence of beeps or calls. Before you go, make sure that everyone is aware of these signs.

Putting the plan into practice

Effective emergency communication requires practice. Plan exercises that mimic possible emergency scenarios. By familiarizing everyone with their responsibilities and the tools, this preparedness will boost self-assurance and lessen anxiety in the event of actual emergencies.

Have your group use their GMRS radios to communicate in a simulated emergency situation. This exercise will enable you to find any holes in your plan and make the required corrections.

Maintaining Flexibility

While having a strategy is crucial, maintaining flexibility is just as crucial. Since circumstances might change quickly, it's critical to be ready to modify your communication approach. Review and revise your strategy frequently in light of lessons discovered from past excursions or modifications to the group's makeup.

Organizing with Neighborhood Emergency Services

Being prepared for emergencies involves more than just your group's actions; it also involves your ability to communicate with emergency services and local authorities. Developing a strong rapport with these organizations might offer an extra degree of security when going on outdoor excursions.

Comprehending local resources

Investigate the local emergency services that are offered in the places you'll be visiting beforehand. Be familiar with the phone numbers of the local search and rescue teams, police, and fire departments. Volunteer fire departments and community emergency response teams (CERT) are also available in many rural areas to help in times of need.

Make sure that everyone in your group has access to the list of these contacts. Make a little emergency card with these numbers on it and give it to every member.

Creating protocols for communication

Being able to successfully interact with these local agencies is crucial in case of an emergency. Here is how to get ready:

• **Understand the Process:** Become familiar with the local emergency reporting process. Certain areas could have unique procedures, such as utilizing specialized radio frequencies to contact emergency assistance.

• **Give Concise and Clear Information:** When speaking with local authorities, give clear and concise information. Please provide your location, emergency type, and any other information that may help responders reach you faster.

• **Follow Up:** It's critical to maintain communication with local agencies following the reporting of an emergency. Inform them of any modifications to the circumstances or your current location. Clear communication can assist them in modifying their response in the event that the incident worsens.

Developing Connections

Before you go, think about building a relationship with the local emergency services. Attend neighborhood gatherings or activities where you can interact with local responders if you frequently visit a particular location. By developing these ties, you can learn more about their resources and the best ways to communicate in an emergency.

Case Studies from Real Life Showing How to Communicate Effectively in Emergencies

Examples from everyday life can highlight how crucial it is to have a communication strategy. Let's look at some examples of successful emergency communication.

First Case Study: The Stormy Trek

A group was caught off guard by an unexpected storm at a well-attended hiking event. Regular check-ins using GMRS radios were part of the communication plan that the leader had put in place. As soon as the storm arrived, the trip leader radioed everyone to tell them to take cover at a ranger station nearby.

Due to their assigned responsibilities, the navigator promptly led everyone to safety, and the communicator maintained contact with nearby emergency services to guarantee assistance was on its way. Preparation kept the group safe and sound by nightfall.

Case Study 2: Disoriented but Not by Himself

In another case, when a youngster went missing, a family camping trip descended into chaos. The parents promptly assigned duties after activating their communication plan. While the other and older siblings looked for the child, one parent remained at the campsite to stay in touch with the local park services.

The parent conducting the search communicated with the campers using their GMRS radios. The family's plan established clear communication, which allowed local rangers to be briefed on the situation as soon as they arrived. Within an hour, the infant was discovered uninjured.

Chapter 7

SolvingTypical Problems

Recognizing and Treating Typical GMR Issues

There is a world of convenience available when using GMRS radios, particularly for outdoor enthusiasts and emergency preparedness advocates. These radios can, however, have a number of problems, just like any other device. Maintaining positive communication when it counts most requires knowing how to recognize and diagnose these issues.

Recognizing typical GMRS issues

Let's start by talking about some common problems you could run across when using your GMRS radio. Early detection of these issues can ultimately save you time and frustration.

1. Signal Loss: Losing the signal is one of the most frequent problems consumers have. This could occur when you pass behind a hill or thicket of trees while hiking. However, malfunctioning equipment or incorrect radio settings might also result in signal loss.

2. Static and Noise: It may be difficult to hear talks clearly if you're experiencing a bothersome crackling sound or static. There are several possible sources of this interference, such as other radios, electrical devices, or ambient air.

3. Poor Audio Quality: Voices may occasionally sound muffled or garbled. A malfunctioning microphone, a dead battery, or misconfigured radio settings could be the cause of this.

4. Power Problems: Occasionally, radios may not switch on or suddenly lose power. Although battery problems are frequently the cause of this issue, it may also be a sign of a more serious electrical issue with the device.

5. Inability to Transmit: It's possible that your radio can pick up signals but won't let you send them. This can be annoying, particularly when communication is crucial in an emergency.

Identifying Problems: A Methodical Approach

Finding the underlying source of an issue is the next step after identifying it. Here's a straightforward method:

1. Examine the Fundamentals: Always begin with the simplest answers. Make sure your radio is turned on and charged. Make sure the squelch setting is set correctly and that you are on the correct channel if it isn't transmitting.

2. Check the antenna: Significant signal loss may result from an antenna that is damaged or connected incorrectly. Make sure there is no obvious damage and that the antenna is firmly attached. Check if replacing the antenna with an extra one fixes the problem.

3. Check the Battery: Poor audio quality and transmission troubles are just two of the problems that can arise from weak or defective batteries. If you're using a rechargeable model, either recharge the device or change the batteries. Keep in mind that older batteries might not be as effective at holding a charge.

4. Keep an eye on the environment: Your radio's performance may occasionally be impacted by outside variables like the weather or topography. Pay attention to these factors and think about how they might affect your conversation.

5. Check for Interference: Look for possible sources of interference if you think there may be noise or static. Signals can be interfered with by nearby electronic devices, such as microwaves and computers. To see if the problem goes away, move to a different area or turn off any nearby electronics.

6. Make a Test Call: After you've mastered the fundamentals, make a test call with a buddy or other radio user. This useful step helps you identify the possible reason and determine whether the issue continues.

Remedies for Interference, Static, and Signal Loss

You can use some techniques to restore clarity and dependability in your GMRS communication when dealing with problems like signal loss, static, and interference.

1. Enhancing the reception of signals

Shift Location: To improve your signal, go to an open space or higher ground. Radio performance can be significantly enhanced by elevation, particularly in steep areas.

Change Your Position: Try moving the radio or yourself if you're having trouble getting a signal in a particular area. Reception can occasionally be enhanced by merely rotating the device a little.

2. Handling Noise and Static

Pick the Correct Channels: Steer clear of crowded channels where interference is likely to occur. To identify a channel with fewer static and congestion, test each one.

Modify the Squelch: This feature aids in reducing background noise. By adjusting it, you can get rid of extraneous static while preserving crucial information.

3. Cutting Down on Interference

Keep Your Equipment Apart: To minimize interference, keep your GMRS radio separate from other electronic devices. The likelihood of static can be considerably reduced by a few feet.

Upgrade Your Antenna: Purchasing a higher-quality antenna could be beneficial if you frequently experience interference. Your signal strength can be increased and noise can be decreased with a high-gain antenna.

GMRS Radio Repair and Maintenance Advice

Many frequent problems can be avoided in the first place with routine maintenance. The following useful advice will help you maintain your GMRS radio in optimal condition:

1. Routine Cleaning: Performance might be hampered by moisture and dirt. Use a soft cloth to clean your radio on a regular basis, paying particular attention to the antenna and connectors. Steer clear of harsh chemicals since they can harm the device.

2. Battery Maintenance: If you won't be using the radio for a long time, always take the batteries out. By doing this, you may avoid battery degradation and make sure your radio is operational when you need it.

3. Software Updates: There are certain GMRS radios that have updated software. Make sure you have the newest features and fixes by routinely checking for manufacturer updates.

4. Store Correctly: Make sure your radio is kept in a dry, temperature-controlled space. Performance problems might result from internal components being damaged by extreme heat or cold.

When to Get Help from a Professional

Sometimes it's best to have professional assistance, even if many problems may be fixed with a little maintenance and troubleshooting.

1. Persistent Issues: If the problem still exists after doing the fundamental checks, it may be a sign of a more serious one. Expert diagnostics can identify issues that you might not be aware of.

2. Electrical Malfunctions: Don't try to fix your radio yourself if it's having electrical problems, including not turning on or overheating. These issues may be dangerous.

3. Parts and repairs Replacement: After extended use, some parts might require replacement. A specialist can guarantee that repairs are completed appropriately, maintaining your device's functioning.

4. Warranty Services: Contact the manufacturer for assistance if your radio is still covered under warranty. It's advisable to get professional assistance because doing repairs on your own could void the guarantee.

Example from the Real World: A Trekking Experience

Imagine being in charge of a group of people going on a mountain hike. You feel the thrill, but your radio keeps cutting out. You recognize the signal loss calmly rather than in a panic. You can get back in contact with your group and coordinate safe trail navigation by relocating to a higher altitude and modifying the squelch.

Chapter 8

Complex GMRS Methods

Examining Digital Modes and Their Uses

Communication has been transformed by digital forms, particularly in outdoor and emergency preparedness contexts. The introduction of digital communication has several benefits, such as improved clarity, mistake correction, and the capacity to send more data in a smaller bandwidth, even though traditional analog channels have been useful to humanity. Your GMRS experience can be greatly enhanced by being aware of these digital modes, which enable more dependable and efficient communication.

Digital Modes: What Are They?

Communication techniques that transform audio and other signals into digital data that may be sent via radio waves are referred to as digital modes. Packet radio, DMR (Digital Mobile Radio), and P25 (Project 25) are examples of common digital modes in GMRS. They are useful tools for both outdoor enthusiasts and emergency personnel because each mode has a distinct function.

1. The packet radio

One of the first methods of digital communication was packet radio. It divides communications into data packets and sends them over radio waves. Particularly in emergency situations where voice communication may be impaired, this mode is great for delivering text messages and providing location data.

For example, a GMRS operator can use packet radio to transmit location coordinates or brief status updates to a central station or other operators during a natural disaster when speech channels would be overloaded. This technique guarantees that important information is transmitted without distortion while simultaneously conserving bandwidth.

2. Digital Mobile Radio, or DMR

DMR is a more recent digital mode that has become more well-liked because of its effective use of frequency and excellent sound quality. In DMR, multiple conversations can occur on the same frequency. This is especially helpful in emergency scenarios where it's critical for several responders to coordinate.

Suppose that during a wildfire, a team of first responders is coordinating their actions. They can efficiently manage resources, exchange updates, and have clear communication with each other without interfering with each other's transmissions by using DMR. Because digital audio is so clear, important information is literally not lost in the din.

Useful implementations in emergencies

Digital modes have a wide range of uses in emergency scenarios. Advocates for emergency preparedness can use these resources to improve communication in times of crisis. Here are some real-world examples:

• **Data Transmission:** Rescuers can utilize packet radio to send environmental data and GPS coordinates back to a command center during a search and rescue operation. This makes it possible to allocate resources and plan effectively.

• **Group Coordination:** Teams can divide into smaller groups while still communicating because of DMR's capacity to support various channels. This function is important when specialized teams may need to work autonomously during large-scale situations but still need to coordinate with the main command.

• **Remote Monitoring:** To keep an eye on the surroundings, sophisticated digital modes can be integrated with distant sensors. This can be particularly helpful in outdoor environments where planning activities or maintaining safety may require real-time information regarding temperature, humidity, or weather changes.

Making use of advanced features

Modern GMRS radios have a number of capabilities that can greatly improve their utility, particularly in emergency and outdoor scenarios. Weather monitoring and GPS integration are two of the most significant functions; both can offer real-time information that is essential for communication and safety.

GPS Integration: Your Helper for Navigation

Picture yourself hiking through a thick forest when all of a sudden you become lost. It can save your life to have a GMRS radio that integrates GPS. With the help of these radios, you can easily locate yourself or find your way back to a pre-arranged spot by sending your GPS coordinates to others.

1. How It Operates

The majority of contemporary GMRS radios have GPS receivers integrated into them that can offer exact location information. Your coordinates are transmitted with your voice or data when you send a message. In addition to improving safety, this feature facilitates group member coordination.

One member of a trekking group, for example, can easily send a distress call and their location if they run into problems and require help. Then, other group members can travel straight to that person's location using their GPS-enabled GMRS radios.

2. Real-world use

• **Search and Rescue Operations:** Having GPS integration enables rescuers to rapidly locate people in distress in situations where time is of the essence. Response times can be significantly shortened by this technology, which may even save lives.

• **Coordination of Outdoor Activities:** Each participant can communicate their GPS location to the group while camping. This is especially helpful in places where standard communication channels might not work, including those with poor mobile reception. People can swiftly help someone who becomes lost or strays too far.

Weather Tracking: Prevent the Storm

The weather can change quickly, particularly outside. In order to help users make well-informed decisions regarding their activities, advanced GMRS radios frequently come equipped with weather monitoring tools that offer real-time information on circumstances.

1. How It Operates

NOAA (National Oceanic and Atmospheric Administration) weather channels, which transmit weather information continuously, are a standard feature of many GMRS radios. Users may be notified by this feature about severe weather alerts or other conditions that could affect their safety.

For instance, your GMRS radio can alert you to severe weather alerts if you're camping in a mountainous region and a storm is approaching. With this instant knowledge, you can take action before the weather worsens, whether that means finding shelter or packing up your tent.

2. Real-world use

• **Safety Alerts:** By warning of approaching storms, flash floods, or strong winds, weather monitoring can help avert hazardous circumstances. Advocates for emergency preparedness can use this tool to protect their families outdoors.

• **Activity Planning:** Outdoor enthusiasts can make better plans for their activities by being aware of the weather prediction. Real-time weather updates guarantee that you're ready for any eventuality, whether you're going on a trek, camping vacation, or fishing expedition.

Your outdoor experience and disaster readiness can be significantly improved by integrating GPS and weather monitoring into your GMRS communication plan. You may stay informed and navigate with confidence by utilizing these sophisticated capabilities, which will guarantee that you're always prepared for whatever nature throws at you.

Integrating other communication technologies with GMRS

Your ability to communicate can be greatly improved by combining GMRS with other communication technologies, particularly for outdoor enthusiasts and emergency preparedness advocates. Even though GMRS radios have outstanding clarity and range, combining them with other technologies can result in a strong communication network that can adjust to different situations. To increase your operational effectiveness, let's examine how to integrate GMR with other systems.

1. Making use of cellular technology

Because cellphones are so common, combining GMRS with cellular technology has the potential to revolutionize the industry. For example, a lot of GMRS radios now have Bluetooth, which lets you pair your radio with your smartphone. In remote locations with poor but still reachable cellular signals, this can enable smooth communication.

Useful Example: Let's say that one of your pals gets lost while trekking with you. In addition to utilizing a mapping tool on your smartphone to find your way back to a prearranged meeting spot, you can use your GMRS radio to communicate with the group. Everyone can stay connected thanks to the combination of cellular and GMRS technologies, particularly in places where cell towers might not be able to reach.

2. Making use of Internet access

A complete communication network can be established by combining GMRS with push-to-talk apps or internet-based communication tools like Zello. Real-time audio communication over the internet is made possible by these apps, which is especially helpful in situations where radios alone might not be adequate or when GMRS channels are crowded.

Real-World Example: First responders frequently experience communication disruptions after natural catastrophes. To improve communication, some organizations have begun combining GMRS radios with apps like Zello. Responders can keep open lines of communication even in situations when the local infrastructure is compromised by using GMRS for coordination on the ground and the app to transmit information back to their operations centers.

3. Making use of satellite communication

Satellite communication systems provide a crucial backup for travelers heading into extremely remote places where cellular and GMRS service are unavailable. You may incorporate gadgets like Iridium satellite phones or Garmin inReach into your communication plan.

Useful Application: Consider a multi-day camping excursion in the mountains where phone coverage is nonexistent and weather conditions change suddenly. You establish a two-tiered safety net by using a satellite device for emergency signals or texting loved ones with updates and a GMRS radio for local communication within your group. For both emergency preparation advocates and outdoor enthusiasts, this redundancy is essential because it guarantees that you may contact for assistance if needed.

4. Using drones and GMRS together

The use of drones in search and rescue missions is growing in popularity. Drones, when combined with GMRS technology, can offer a distinct viewpoint and useful situational awareness. Certain drones can be fitted with GMRS radios, which enable teams on the ground to communicate in real time.

Case Study: A drone with a GMRS radio was used in a recent case study that involved a search and rescue mission in a mountainous area. It sent live footage to the command center while conducting aerial surveillance of the region. Based on the drone's findings, the ground team coordinated their search operations using GMRS radios. By giving the rescuers vital information about the terrain and possible dangers, this technological combination not only improved the operation's efficiency but also increased their safety.

5. Combining Ham Radio and GMRS

Combining GMRS and ham radio can be beneficial for people who want to increase their communication capabilities even more. Greater range and a variety of frequency bands that GMRS alone might not provide are two advantages of ham radios.

Practical Application: While ham radios manage cooperation with local law enforcement or emergency services, GMRS can be utilized for local communications among event staff during huge events, like a marathon or a community festival. This multi-tiered strategy can guarantee that all parties are in agreement and that communications are efficient and transparent.

6. Using Mesh Systems

GMRS systems can also be integrated with mesh networking technology. Every device functions as a node in a decentralized communication system created by mesh networks. It is a reliable option for both emergency and outdoor situations since even if one node fails, the others can still communicate.

Real-World Example: During a community readiness drill, GMRS radios and a mesh network enabled numerous participants to communicate over a wide region without depending on a central hub. In rural locations with little traditional communication infrastructure, this is extremely advantageous. By exchanging information, each participant might build a more extensive network of communication for all parties.

Case Studies on Creative Applications of GMRS

Examining creative applications of GMRS technology demonstrates its adaptability and efficiency in practical settings. Gaining insight from these case studies will encourage outdoor enthusiasts and disaster preparedness advocates to use GMRS in innovative ways that improve communication and safety.

1. Emergency Response Teams in the Community (CERTs)

GMRS radios have been successfully used by Community Emergency Response Teams in a number of locations for both training and real-world crisis situations. In times of crisis, whether natural disasters or local catastrophes, these volunteer organizations are prepared to support local emergency services.

Case Study: A local CERT provided GMRS radios to its members during a period of severe floods. They coordinated neighborhood evacuation activities and built contact lines with nearby emergency agencies. A more coordinated reaction and the saving of lives were made possible by the prompt and effective transmission of critical information made possible by the usage of GMRS.

2. Adventure Racing

Running, cycling, and kayaking are just a few of the outdoor sports that are combined in adventure racing. Teams competing in these races frequently encounter difficulties where prompt communication is essential.

Case Study: To stay in touch over a variety of terrain during a recent adventure race, one team decided to use GMRS radios. They faced challenges as the race went on, including injuries and poor navigation. They were able to get help and promptly update race organizers on their situation thanks to GMRS. In addition to keeping them safe, their strategic use of GMRS radios enabled medical teams to intervene promptly.

3. Handling Wildfires

Effective communication is crucial for managing and responding to outbreaks in wildfire-prone areas. GMRS radios are being used more and more by emergency responders and firefighters to coordinate field operations.

Case Study: Ground crews with GMRS radios were able to stay in touch with air support teams during a major wildfire. This made it possible for them to communicate information in real time on resource requirements, topographical risks, and fire sites. Incorporating GMRS technology into their operations enhanced response times and coordination, which eventually contributed to more effective fire control.

Chapter 9

Real-World Uses of GMRS Parts

Camping, hiking, and off-roading are examples of recreational activities that provide the ideal setting for taking in the wonderful outdoors, but they also pose particular communication issues. As a supporter of disaster preparedness or an outdoor enthusiast, having a dependable way to stay connected can improve your travels while guaranteeing security and friendship. GMRS radios are a notable option that bridges the gap between enjoyment and usefulness.

Recreational activities: off-roading, hiking, and camping

Imagine yourself isolated from the outside world while camping beneath a starry sky and surrounded by the sounds of nature, only to find out that your phone's battery is dead. Outdoor enthusiasts are all too familiar with this situation. Without depending on cellular signals, GMRS radios can offer that crucial connection, enabling you to speak with loved ones, friends, or other campers.

Selecting the proper GMRS radio

Choosing the appropriate GMRS radio is essential. Think of lightweight, portable devices with high battery life for trekking and camping. Look for tools that can alert you to impending storms or changes in the weather, such as weather alerts. Multiple channel models will make it simple for you to change frequencies in order to prevent interference from other groups and guarantee uninterrupted communication.

Useful advice for effective communication

Assign each group member a specific channel before setting out on a hiking excursion. In addition to making communication easier, this structure keeps conversation in order. For example, you could assign the group leader to Channel 1, the hiker in the back to Channel 2, and everyone else to Channel 3. Confusion is avoided, and check-ins are made simple with clear classifications.

My party recently experienced an unforeseen weather shift while camping. We had to swiftly decide whether to stay or pack things as dark clouds crept in. "This is Base Camp," the group leader said over GMRS. A storm is approaching. Check in, everyone. We were able to swiftly evaluate our options and relocate to safety since each member replied with their location and status. This example shows how GMRS improves decision-making and coordination in leisure situations.

Being ready for emergencies in recreational environments

Additionally, GMRS radios are crucial for emergency preparedness. Being able to communicate can save lives in the event of an accident or other unforeseen circumstance in a distant area. To be prepared for anything the wilderness may throw at you, bring a small first aid kit with your radio.

Imagine a situation in which a hiker kilometers from the trailhead twists their ankle. One person can stay behind to aid, and another can call for assistance using the GMRS radio. By giving vital information about your position and the nature of the emergency, this prompt communication can make all the difference.

Community Involvement: Local Events and Neighborhood Watch

Beyond personal exploration, GMRS radios excel in contexts that foster community involvement, such as local events and neighborhood watch programs. GMRS provides a strong platform for bringing neighbors together and encouraging cooperation as communities cooperate to improve safety and communication.

Starting a Community Watch

GMRS radios are being used in several neighborhoods to increase resident safety and coordination. Getting interested neighbors together and providing them with GMRS radios can be the first step in starting a neighborhood watch organization. Establish a specific channel for community communication so that locals may easily plan neighborhood events or report suspicious activity.

For instance, a neighborhood in my region activated their GMRS communication plan after a recent rise in local crime. Residents started doing routine check-ins and assigned Channel 5 to watch members. The neighborhood was able to move immediately to ensure safety and peace of mind after one person radioed in to report any strange activity.

Organizing events in the community

Additionally, GMRS radios help improve neighborhood gatherings like fairs, block parties, and fundraisers. To improve communication and the overall experience, give radios to volunteers, event coordinators, and security guards. When it comes to organizing logistics, handling emergencies, or directing traffic, this approach guarantees that everyone is in agreement.

For instance, GMRS radios were used by event planners to coordinate events during a local charity run. Effective communication was essential to the event's success, from guiding participants to the starting line to making sure first aid stations were stocked and prepared. Volunteers kept everyone informed and secure by communicating information in a timely and effective manner.

The Strength of Social Bonds

Communities can improve safety, forge bonds, and provide a supportive atmosphere by encouraging communication via GMRS radios. GMRS can contribute to the strengthening of the community's fabric by encouraging a sense of duty and belonging as neighbors bond over common issues and experiences.

GMRS radios are empowered to change neighborhood dynamics and outdoor experiences through recreational use and community involvement. In addition to improving your own experiences, putting an emphasis on open communication makes the community safer, more knowledgeable, and more connected.

Group and Family Emergency Preparedness

Having a fully filled kit is only one aspect of emergency readiness; another is making sure that you and your loved ones can communicate clearly when it counts most. In these circumstances, GMRS radios are indispensable instruments that provide a dependable way to remain in contact. In times of crisis, good communication can mean the difference between turmoil and peace for families and groups. Let's discuss how to use GMRS to enhance your family's preparedness strategy.

1. Establishing a Plan for Communication

Creating a thorough communication strategy is the first step in emergency preparation. Who will utilize GMRS radios, how they will communicate, and what information will be communicated should all be specified in this strategy. Here's how you develop a successful communication plan:

• **Identify Key Users:** Choose the members of your family or group who will be equipped with a GMRS radio. Verify that everyone is able to use the gadget.

• **Designate Channels:** Select particular channels for various circumstances. Use one channel for routine check-ins and another for emergencies, for instance. This prevents misunderstandings and guarantees that important information is conveyed unhindered.

• **Create Protocols:** Create a set of guidelines for communicating in case of an emergency. For example, choose a quick way to communicate information. "This is Camp Alpha," someone would say if they saw a possible threat. We would like an update on the possible problem at the lake. Over.

2. Practice sessions and drills

It's crucial to practice your communication strategy. Everyone can feel more at ease using GMRS radios under pressure with regular training. Plan drills that replicate actual emergency situations. Here's a useful strategy:

• **Scenario-Based Drills:** Construct hypothetical situations, including an unexpected thunderstorm or a child going missing. Consider, for example, a scenario in which a hiker becomes separated. Ask everyone to practice checking in, finding the missing person, and organizing a search using their radios.

Assign roles to members of your family or group through roleplaying. Assign one somebody, for instance, to be the "lead communicator," in charge of obtaining data and guiding activities. This guarantees that everyone is aware of their roles in an emergency and fosters the development of leadership abilities.

3. Being aware of GMRS's limitations

Despite their strength, it's important to recognize the limitations of GMRS radios. Learn about the geography and distance, for example, that can affect communication. Here are some important things to think about:

• **Terrain Difficulties:** Signals may be blocked by hills, dense forests, or structures. Practice utilizing GMRS in several places to determine where the strongest signals are if you're in an area with large elevation variations.

• **Range Considerations:** In open spaces, GMRS radios can usually reach up to five miles, but in populated or forested regions, their range can be greatly diminished. In your communication plan, note these restrictions and make backup plans in case the radios malfunction.

4. Communication and emergency situations

Effective communication can save lives in emergency situations. The following useful advice can help you use GMRS in a variety of scenarios:

• **Natural disasters:** Keep yourself updated and stay in touch with your loved ones during situations like hurricanes or wildfires. Assign a "designated communicator" to monitor developments and make sure that everyone is informed. As an illustration, "This is Camp Bravo." We've been informed that a storm is on its way. We must move to a higher location. Over.

Medical Emergencies: Call for assistance using your GMRS if you are hurt or experiencing health problems. Establish unambiguous signals, such as a particular code or phrase, for medical crises. "This is Camp Delta," for example. A medical emergency has arisen. Asking for help. Over.

5. Including Kids in the Preparation Process

It can be uplifting and essential for family safety to teach kids how to operate GMRS radios. Here's how to interact with them:

• **Age-appropriate Training:** Adapt your instruction to the participants' developmental stage. While older children can practice more complicated speech, younger toddlers can learn how to call for aid. Make learning enjoyable by using role-playing games.

• **Developing confidence:** During family vacations or neighborhood gatherings, encourage them to practice operating the radios. This boosts their self-esteem and makes sure they're ready to speak clearly in case of an emergency.

Examining GMRS's Function in Workplace Environments

GMRS radios provide a flexible means of efficient communication in business settings. Their dependable connectivity makes them useful not only for outdoor enthusiasts but also for emergency services, corporations, and educational institutions. Safety and operational effectiveness can be improved by comprehending the function of GMRS in these situations.

1. Business correspondence

For smooth communication, many businesses, particularly those that operate in large spaces or outdoors, can use GMRS radios. These radios are useful for streamlining operations, whether you're handling logistics in a big warehouse or organizing a building site. Here's how to make the most of them:

• **Team Coordination:** Give each team a specific channel. For example, a safety team may watch one channel while a construction crew uses another for regular operations. This group makes sure that everyone may speak without being interrupted and reduces chatter.

• **Emergency Procedures:** Define precise procedures for communicating in case of an emergency. This can involve making quick calls for help in the event of mishaps or equipment malfunctions. For instance, "Site Alpha is this." A safety incident has occurred. requesting an urgent response. Over.

2. Organizing Events

GMRS radios are essential for organizing activities and guaranteeing safety during events like fairs, festivals, and community get-togethers. Here's how to successfully put these into practice:

• **Real-Time Communication:** Give staff members in charge of different regions of the event radios. This makes it possible to provide prompt updates on emergency situations, vendor cooperation, and crowd management.

• **Fast Reactions:** Employees are able to communicate information quickly in the event of an emergency, such as a medical situation or a security concern. "This is Event Control," for instance. At the main stage, there is a medical emergency. Respond, medical staff. Over.

3. Academic establishments

GMRS radios are extremely useful for schools, especially when they are going on field excursions or doing outside activities. Maintaining communication between staff and teachers guarantees both efficient coordination and student safety.

• **Student Monitoring:** During outside activities, give teachers radios. They are able to discuss any worries, guaranteeing a prompt resolution of any possible problems. "This is Teacher Bravo," for instance. Two students are missing, and we need to find them. Over.

• **Emergency Drills:** Include the use of GMRS in emergency exercises. To become comfortable with the radios' features, staff and students should practice utilizing them in a variety of situations, like lockdowns or evacuations.

4. Emergency Services and Public Safety

GMRS radios are essential for emergency response and public safety. The dependable communication that these gadgets offer is advantageous to law enforcement, firefighters, and emergency medical personnel.

• **Coordinated Responses:** GMRS radios let authorities communicate with one another during crises, like natural disasters or major occurrences. By ensuring that everyone is in agreement, this improves efficiency and speeds up response times.

• **Training and Drills:** GMRS usage should be covered in emergency services' training courses. Frequent exercises guarantee that all staff members are conversant with the radios and capable of using them efficiently in actual crises.

Chapter 10

Comprehending GMRS Law and Upcoming Developments

Synopsis of Current GMRS Rules and Updates on Licenses

The General Mobile Radio Service (GMRS) environment is constantly shifting due to both changing user demands and regulatory frameworks. Understanding the present and upcoming GMRS standards is essential for outdoor enthusiasts and emergency preparedness advocates to ensure safe and efficient communication in the field.

An overview of the most recent licensing updates and GMRS regulations

In the US, GMRS is subject to particular rules established by the Federal Communications Commission (FCC). According to current revisions, operating on GMRS frequencies still requires a GMRS license, but the procedure has been simplified to make it simpler to obtain one. The main elements of the present GMRS regulations are as follows:

1. License prerequisites:

The FCC requires a license for everyone who wants to use GMRS. With this license, users can broadcast on GMRS frequencies between 462.550 and 467.725 MHz. Crucially, a GMRS license enables the whole family to operate GMRS radios without requiring individual permits.

The licensing price is currently $70 and is good for ten years. Anyone interested in using GMRS for emergency or personal communications can use it because there are no exams needed.

2. Allocation of Frequencies:

GMRS frequencies are separated into channels, some of which are shared with FRS channels. However, GMRS radios are the better option for people who require dependable communication over longer distances because they have higher power and a longer range than FRS radios.

3. Power Limitations:

Compared to FRS, GMRS permits higher power limitations, with a maximum permitted power of 50 watts. Users must, however, respect certain channel power limitations, especially when sharing frequencies with FRS. It is crucial to comprehend these boundaries in order to guarantee adherence and peak performance.

4. Etiquette and Interference:

Users should observe appropriate radio etiquette and refrain from interfering with other services. This entails identifying oneself, communicating clearly, and avoiding channel monopolization. Being a thoughtful operator contributes to keeping the atmosphere favorable for all GMRS users.

Staying up to date with these rules guarantees that users are in compliance, which is crucial for community standards and individual safety.

The Function of GMRS in Emergency Services and Its Future

GMRS appears to have a bright future, especially as the need for dependable communication in emergency situations increases. GMRS's function in emergency services is changing, and some significant developments are showing up:

1. Combining Different Technologies:

As technology develops, GMRS is probably going to become increasingly integrated with cellphones and digital communication systems. For instance, situational awareness can be improved during emergencies by utilizing GMRS radios in conjunction with applications that offer position tracking and emergency notifications. GMRS may become a more effective emergency preparedness tool as a result of this collaboration.

2. Enhanced utilization in Emergencies:

The importance of GMRS in disaster response and recovery is becoming more widely acknowledged by emergency responders and community organizations. GMRS might be an essential lifeline in the event that conventional communication systems malfunction. In an emergency, users can easily create networks for information sharing, rescue coordination, and staying in touch with loved ones.

3. Programs for Community Preparedness:

GMRS training is now a part of many communities' preparedness initiatives. Communities can become more resilient to emergencies, public safety incidents, and natural disasters by teaching residents how to use GMRS efficiently. These initiatives enable people and families to take preventative measures to protect themselves.

4. Support for GMRS:

Campaigns to encourage the use of GMRS are probably going to get up steam. Community leaders and organizations may advocate for increased resources and policies that encourage trustworthy communication as more people realize how important it is. In addition to enhancing GMRS services, lobbying promotes a feeling of community involvement.

Emergency preparedness advocates and outdoor enthusiasts can effectively utilize GMRS and make sure they are prepared to communicate in an emergency by keeping up with its laws and understanding its possibilities. Beyond personal use, GMRS's practical uses establish it as an essential instrument for resilience and community safety in a world that is becoming more unpredictable.

Communication Technology Trends Affecting GMRS

The GMRS (General Mobile Radio Service) landscape changes in tandem with advancements in communication technologies. In addition to changing the way we communicate, the current changes affecting GMRS are also influencing the foundation of disaster preparedness. To keep ahead of the curve, outdoor enthusiasts and emergency preparedness advocates must comprehend these shifts.

Communication technology trends are affecting GMRS

1. Developments in Digital Communication

Digital communication has revolutionized analog communication. Digital features like encryption and better sound quality are being added to GMRS radios more often. Users can send brief messages without requiring a full discussion because of digital modes' text messaging capabilities and improved intelligibility. This can result in a more dependable connection when it counts most for outdoor enthusiasts venturing into isolated regions.

Example from the Real World: Let's say you are trekking in a national park. While keeping your hands free to navigate, a digital GMRS radio lets you quickly SMS your group to let them know you're traveling a different track.

2. Smartphone Integration

Another noteworthy trend is the incorporation of GMRS technology into cell phones. These days, several GMRS radios have Bluetooth built in, making it simple to connect to mobile devices. This improves situational awareness in outdoor settings by enabling users to get GPS, maps, and even weather updates straight through their radios.

Realistic Suggestion: Take into account purchasing a GMRS radio that is capable of syncing with your smartphone. By improving communication and providing vital information, this feature will keep you ready for whatever your adventures bring.

3. The value of emergency communications has increased.

GMRS is playing an increasingly important role in emergency communications as natural catastrophes become more frequent and severe. GMRS networks are being established by numerous towns as a component of their emergency response strategies. This pattern emphasizes how important it is to have skilled operators who can use GPS technology in an emergency.

Engagement Tip: To learn how GMRS can be included in your community's disaster response plans, attend training sessions or local emergency preparedness groups. You can help keep your neighborhood safe by learning about these networks.

Promoting GMRS and Community Engagement

1. Increasing knowledge and awareness.

For GMRS technology to continue to advance and be adopted, advocacy is essential. Your voices are crucial in highlighting the advantages of GMRS as outdoor lovers and emergency preparation advocates. The capabilities of GMRS and its significance in emergency scenarios are still not widely known. Organizing seminars or educational meetings might assist in spreading awareness of the benefits of GMRS radio use.

Advocacy Example: Planning a community gathering with an emergency preparedness theme can be a wonderful way to introduce GMRS. Invite emergency services, outdoor organizations, and local radio clubs to speak about the advantages and real-world uses of GMRS.

2. Promoting involvement in local networks

Promoting involvement in local GMRS networks is another crucial component of campaigning. In order to increase communication range in emergency situations, many regions are starting to install GMRS repeaters. Participation from the community in these networks improves communication and fosters a sense of readiness by strengthening member camaraderie.

Engagement Idea: Look for GMRS clubs or groups in your area. Many hold frequent gatherings where participants can exchange stories, hone their radio abilities, and talk about rules and technological advancements. This is a fantastic method to remain informed and in touch.

3. Having an Impact on Law and Policy

Regulations that impact GMRS users may be improved by keeping up with GMRS legislation and actively engaging in advocacy initiatives. Knowing how to interact with legislators as outdoor lovers can help influence future communication guidelines and guarantee that GMRS continues to be a practical choice for individual and public safety.

Action Step: Send a letter to your local representatives emphasizing the value of GMRS in outdoor communication and disaster preparedness. A strong argument for ongoing support and development of GMRS can be made by sharing anecdotes or statistics on its effects.

4. Promoting a preparedness community

In the end, GMRS advocacy is about creating a community of knowledgeable, equipped people who are ready to support one another in times of need, not simply about the technology. Urge friends and neighbors to purchase GMRS radios and impart their expertise on efficient communication techniques.

Community Challenge: Establish a local preparation club where members may debate local emergency plans, organize exercises, and exchange advice on how to use GMRS. A resilient community is one that is interconnected.

Chapter 11

Materials and Additional Education

Anyone who wants to learn more about GMRS radio communication must interact with the appropriate internet forums and resources. For outdoor enthusiasts and disaster preparation advocates, gaining access to high-quality resources and interacting with informed people may greatly improve your abilities and self-assurance. This thorough guide will assist you in navigating this vast terrain.

Suggested Internet discussion boards and communities

Online communities and forums are informational gold mines. They offer forums for exchanging insights, resolving problems, and talking about best practices. Here are some highly recommended items:

1. QRZ.com

One of the most extensive amateur radio forums is QRZ.com, which has a special area for GMRS users. Discussions about tools, methods, and user experiences can be found here. Talking with other enthusiasts can help you learn about real-world uses, typical problems, and creative fixes.

2. The Radio Reference Website

There is a large forum on this website dedicated to radio lovers. The GMRS section is active, with users exchanging advice on emergency planning tactics, equipment inspections, and proper communication. In addition to broadening your knowledge, participating in these conversations puts you in touch with knowledgeable users who may provide priceless guidance.

3. Groups on Facebook

There are numerous Facebook groups devoted to emergency communications and GMRS. Groups like "Emergency Communications Enthusiasts" and "GMRS Operators" are excellent for interacting with other users in your area, sharing resources, and having real-time discussions. Members of these platforms are frequently eager to contribute their personal stories, which makes learning more dynamic and relatable.

4. r/GMRS on Reddit

A vibrant community for GMRS aficionados may be found in the r/GMRS subreddit. Users talk about new technology, exchange success stories, and submit queries. A well-rounded perspective on GMRS usage is provided by the relaxed yet educational setting, which welcomes a range of viewpoints.

5. Get-together groups

Look for nearby Meetup groups that are geared toward emergency preparedness, or GMRS. These organizations frequently hold field exercises, talks, and training events that might improve your practical experience. In-person interactions with other enthusiasts can also lead to enduring friendships and joint outdoor adventure opportunities.

Extra reading and reference resources

There are a ton of reading materials available to help you learn more about GMRS in addition to online forums. The following articles and books are suggested:

1. Michael R. Smith's "The Complete Handbook of Portable Radios"

This book provides information on how to use and care for a variety of portable radios, including GMRS. It offers helpful hints and troubleshooting guidance to help consumers make the most of their gadgets.

2. John McGowan's "Emergency Radio Communications for Amateur Radio Operators"

Despite its amateur radio concentration, this book offers fundamental ideas that are pertinent to GMRS users, particularly in emergency situations. It goes over procedures, equipment selections, and situational awareness techniques that come in very handy during emergencies.

3. Steven Smith's "GMRS Radio for Dummies"

An excellent introduction that simplifies the intricacies of GMRS in a friendly manner. It is the ideal companion for both inexperienced and seasoned users because it covers everything from the fundamental functions to sophisticated communication strategies.

4. Publications of the National Emergency Management Agency (NEMA)

A number of documents published by NEMA provide guidelines for emergency communications, including the use of GMRS in disaster situations. Anyone interested in strengthening their emergency preparedness tactics can benefit from their offerings.

5. E-books and online courses

Online courses on disaster preparedness and radio communication are available on platforms such as Coursera and Udemy. These classes frequently feature community discussions and video lectures that can greatly improve your comprehension of GMRS usage.

6. The GMRS Regulations of the FCC

Understanding the rules set forth by the Federal Communications Commission (FCC) regarding GMRS is essential. Official material outlining GMRS users' legal obligations, operational rules, and license requirements can be found on the FCC website.

Participating in these online forums and resources can help you develop a network of people who share your enthusiasm for communication and readiness, in addition to improving your technical proficiency. In addition to improving your personal experiences, the knowledge you acquire may be vital for the security and welfare of those in your immediate vicinity during crises or outdoor pursuits.

Keep in mind that learning never ends as you go through these materials. Every encounter, whether virtual or face-to-face, broadens your knowledge and makes you a more capable and assured GMRS user. As you develop within this lively group, embrace the journey and don't be afraid to connect, ask questions, and share your own ideas.

GMRS-related organizations and agencies

Mastering your radio equipment is only one aspect of understanding GMRS (General Mobile Radio Service); another is utilizing the abundance of information offered by many agencies and organizations. These tools can help you meet like-minded people, improve your abilities, and stay up-to-date on changes in regulations. Here, we'll look at some of the most important groups that can help you learn GMRS, especially for outdoor activities and disaster preparedness.

1. the FCC, or Federal Communications Commission

In the United States, radio communications, including GMRS, are governed by the FCC. Comprehensive details on licenses, norms, and regulations pertaining to the use of GMRS are available on their website. For compliance and efficient operation, it is essential to comprehend these regulations.

• The FCC GMRS Information website

The frequencies designated for GMRS use, the particular regulations for operation, and information about acquiring a GMRS license are all available here. For emergency preparedness advocates who might need to use GMRS in disaster scenarios, it is especially important to stay up to date on any revisions or changes to the regulations.

2. The ARRL, or American Radio Relay League

One of the most well-known associations for amateur radio operators is the ARRL, which also offers GMRS users useful tools. Even though the primary focus is amateur radio, many of the knowledge and skill areas are also applicable to GMRS usage.

• ARRL's website

The ARRL provides training materials, educational materials, and a multitude of articles about radio communication. For outdoor enthusiasts who want to improve their abilities in practical settings, they also have local groups that may offer courses and hands-on training.

3. CBROs, or Citizens Band Radio Operators

The CBRO community frequently overlaps with GMRS users, despite being primarily focused on Citizen Band (CB) radio, especially in outdoor and disaster preparedness circumstances. Members with GMRS experience are also present in several CBRO forums and groups, offering a wide network of support and expertise.

• CB Radio Operator's website

You can meet seasoned users with firsthand knowledge of handling communications during emergencies by joining these communities. They offer advice, hints, and anecdotes that might enlighten and motivate you.

4. Regional Emergency Response Organizations

For GMRS users who are prepared, establishing a connection with nearby emergency management organizations can yield priceless resources. These organizations frequently hold community gatherings, conferences, and training sessions with the goal of enhancing communication in emergency situations.

• **Advice:** Inquire about available training or resources by contacting the emergency management agency in your city or county. You can also improve your comprehension of how GMRS fits into more comprehensive emergency response plans by participating in local exercises or drills.

GMRS User Workshops, Training, and Certifications

Your GMRS knowledge and abilities can be improved by taking part in workshops, training courses, and certifications. In addition to giving you practical experience, these opportunities let you connect with other GMRS users and industry experts.

1. webinars and online courses

Numerous organizations provide webinars and online courses on emergency preparedness, GMRS communication methods, and associated technology. Both novice and expert users can find courses on platforms like Coursera, Udemy, and even websites that specialize in radio.

Take the "Emergency Communications with GMRS" course, for instance, which discusses how to utilize GMRS radios practically in everyday situations. These classes are available to people with hectic schedules because they may frequently be finished at your own pace.

2. Local clubs for amateur radio

One of the best ways to get involved in the radio community is to join a local amateur radio club. Many of these clubs provide workshops and training sessions designed especially for GMRS users, giving them firsthand experience with the tools and real-world situations.

Clubs frequently organize field days where you can get experience assembling and using your GMRS equipment under different circumstances. For outdoor enthusiasts who like to make sure they're ready for everything, this practical experience can be quite beneficial.

3. Programs for Certification

Getting a general amateur radio license can greatly improve your knowledge and abilities, even if GMRS does not require a specialized certification like some other radio services do. Numerous training courses provide you with a strong foundation in radio theory and operation and prepare you for the technician or general-class amateur radio tests.

To assist you in passing the licensure examinations, groups such as the ARRL and other local clubs frequently offer study guides, practice tests, and workshops. This certification broadens your knowledge of communication concepts that are applicable to GMRS usage in addition to increasing your capabilities as a radio operator.

4. Emergency Response Teams in the Community (CERT)

Enrolling in CERT programs can offer vital emergency preparedness training, which includes communication techniques. These initiatives, which are usually run by local governments, teach people how to help in an emergency.

Being a member of a CERT team as a GMRS user allows you to immediately apply your knowledge to practical situations. You'll discover how to work with emergency services, communicate effectively in emergency situations, and support your community in times of crisis.

Example from the Real World: A Useful Workshop

Consider enrolling in your local emergency management agency's GMRS communication workshop. During the first part of the day, you will receive practical instruction on how to set up your radio equipment, optimize its settings, and practice using appropriate communication etiquette.

There is a simulated emergency, and you have to discuss safety procedures with your staff. In addition to gaining useful skills, this experience helps you connect with other participants who share your dedication to readiness. You feel powerful after the session, having gained knowledge and a network of people who can help you.

Chapter 12

Concluding Remarks and Upcoming Actions

Summary of the Main Ideas Discussed in the Book

Gaining proficiency in GMRS radio communication has given you the essential abilities and information to handle the challenges of efficient radio use, particularly in emergency situations or outside environments. Let's review the key ideas that have influenced your comprehension and preparedness as we wrap up.

Knowing the Fundamentals of GMRS

We began by going over the basics of General Mobile Radio Service (GMRS), including the differences between it and Family Radio Service (FRS). You can better appreciate the full range of GMRS's offerings if you are aware of the frequencies, power restrictions, and license requirements. Keep in mind that GMRS radios are made for serious communication; they are perfect for outdoor enthusiasts who travel to far-flung locations and for emergency preparation advocates who want to stay in touch in case of an emergency.

Best practices and etiquette in communication

Communication etiquette was one of the key topics discussed. Talking is only one aspect of effective communication; another is listening carefully and giving intelligent answers. We talked about the value of using precise language, accurately employing the terms "over" and "out," and identifying oneself when transmitting. In addition to improving your communication, these techniques will guarantee clarity under pressure.

Procedures and situations for emergencies

It was essential to know how to communicate in an emergency. From planning evacuations during natural catastrophes to staying in touch with loved ones while on outdoor adventures, we explored particular scenarios. The significance of maintaining composure was highlighted by the real-world situations given, such as handling an unexpected weather change when camping. These procedures are lifelines that can guarantee safety in emergency situations; they are more than just rules.

Tools and Upkeep

Another crucial component was familiarity with the actual equipment. We talked about the characteristics of different GMRS radios and how to keep them operating at their best. Miscommunication at critical times can be avoided with helpful advice on battery management, signal strengthening, and common problem-solving techniques.

Promotion of ongoing education and practice

Both your journey and the field of radio communication are always changing. You wouldn't expect to be a great athlete without practice; mastering GMRS takes constant effort. Remember that each radio operation improves your skills.

Engage in local forums or user groups for GMRS. You'll find a community of people that share your enthusiasm for communication in addition to staying current on the newest methods and tools. You will be inspired, challenged, and pushed to consider new concepts when you interact with other people.

Request to Interact with the GMRS Community

In relation to the community, joining the GMRS network can significantly improve your expertise and understanding. Numerous tools are accessible, including social media groups, online forums, and local clubs where fans congregate to exchange advice, insights, and experiences.

Think about going to local amateur radio events or workshops. Making connections with knowledgeable GMRS users can yield information that books might not offer. Additionally, these events frequently provide hands-on opportunities to try out new tools or methods as well as practical demonstrations.

Putting What You've Learnt Into Practice

The time has come for you to apply all of the knowledge you have gained about GMRS radio communication. Set up your GMRS radio and become acquainted with its functions first. Practice with loved ones by acting out different situations that could arise during emergencies or outdoor activities.

Instead of waiting for an emergency to put your abilities to the test, make time to practice. Make sure to utilize your radio whether you're going on a family camping trip or a casual hike. Create procedures for your organization, communicate clearly, and work through problems as a team.

The biggest shift occurs when you put what you've learned into practice. As you prepare for unexpected situations or go into the wild, keep in mind that effective communication can make all the difference. Now is the time to grab your radio, make connections, and confidently embrace the art of communication. Your biggest protection is preparedness, which changes how you enjoy being outside and handle situations.

www.ingramcontent.com/pod-product-compliance
Lightning Source LLC
Chambersburg PA
CBHW060156060326
40690CB00018B/4138